LULU PUBLISHING

GOOGLE'LIZE YOUR LIFE

Jeff VanDrimmelen is a national productivity expert and has been a speaker and presenter from California to North Carolina to New York for organizations such as Educause, The Korea Society of America, The University of North Carolina at Chapel Hill and many other local and international groups. He is a teacher at heart and has taught at the high school and collegiate level and holds a MA and a MBA. He conducts productivity workshops for individuals and businesses around the world. He lives in Dallas, Texas.

GOOGLE'LIZE
Your Life!
Simple and Focused gProductivity

*In other words: Making
technology do all it should do
so you can do what you want to do.*

Jeff VanDrimmelen

LULU PUBLISHING

LULU PUBLISHING

http://lulu.com

Jeff VanDrimmelen

GOOGLE'LIZE Your Life: Simple and Focused gProductivity

ISBN: 978-0-557-49133-9

1. Time Management. 2. Self-management (Psychology).

Printed in the United States of America
Design by Giancarlo Deleon

To my wonderful and amazing companion, Debbi. You and our wonderful kids are the reason I work hard and try to be productive.

Acknowledgements

I would like to thank the many people that have helped me hone and develop my *GOOGLE'LIZE Your Life* system: Randall Huebner for showing me the power of technology in my life; to Zachary Fisher for making me think critically about technology productivity, and teaching by my side as I worked this system out; and Bobby Blankenship for deep thoughts over lunches as we explore the nature of man in today's technology driven world.

Additionally, none of this would have happened without the hundreds of people that have come to my productivity workshops over the years. Your comments, thoughts, struggles, and passions have pushed me to find new and creative ways to harness the power of technology to really help me be productive. Here is the book you have been asking for.

Contents

Introduction

I remember when I got my first calendar. I was that geeky kid...yes, you know the one I'm talking about. The one that carried around a Daytimer® in middle school. I was involved with way too many things and found strange satisfaction in journaling the events of the day. My Daytimer® was my first productivity system. I spent the next decade trying out different paper calendar systems and organizing my (in retrospect) simple life.

Then one day in the mid 90's something amazing happened. My grandpa visited, and he had a new electronic calendar. (My grandpa has always been *very* progressive and introduced me to the latest and greatest gadgets.) I believe it was some sort of proprietary Sony® device, if my memory serves me correctly. I was amazed as he explained how he could enter *as many events* as he wanted *and all* of his contact *and* notes for events. I was in love with the possibilities, and thus began my life-long love affair with technological productivity, as well as the epic battle...paper vs. digital.

All of this happened before we even had the complexity and information overload of the Internet, e-mail, instant messaging, and Twitter®. Over the years, I have tried just about every different combination of paper, computer, and digital device I could. I have changed and honed my system depending on the current device and current employer. I have tired integrated productivity systems, websites, and just about everything under the sun. In the end I have found a system that works for me, and it works well. I have become a Google fanboy. Let me explain.

Why Google?

Eventually my passion for productivity and technology lead me to become a technology trainer. I've been doing personal and group technology productivity consulting for the past 10 years and have seen and trained on just about every software, paper, and productivity system out there. In the end I keep coming back to Google because they just get it. They understand how our minds work and set up systems that are intuitive to us. Instead of focusing on business workflows and needs; they are focused on the individual and designing systems to meet our needs.

I once talked with a Google employee about their Google task system, and as we talked, three points came up that describe *all* Google products. I have summarized them and adopted them as the principles of the *GOOGLE'LIZE Your Life* book.

GOOGLE'LIZE Your Life Principles

#1 Easy and Simple

There shouldn't be a huge learning curve when learning new software. Anyone should be able to just figure out how to use with minimal instructional. People want to be able to get in, do what they need to do, and get out. This is, in fact, what really drew me to Google products. They *are* easy to use.

2 Ubiquity – Available Everywhere

How many platforms do you use? Originally, it was a case of PC vs. Mac. Mobile technologies expanded that. You can't be limited to a single platform. The world doesn't work like that anymore. If you want to be able to access your task list on your mobile phone, it shouldn't matter if you have an iPhone®, a Blackberry®, or a simple phone. You should be able to view, move, delete, and change your email, tasks, calendar items, and all the rest of your information anywhere, easily.

#3 Flexible

Google wants their products to be flexible enough to be used in all the different ways that users would want and need, not just the way they thought it should be used. This could be anything from the simplest task list to the most complex combination of multiple context lists and categories.

"GOOGLE'LIZE" – The Verb

Today, the verb "google" means so much more than looking up something with Google's search engine. It now means to look up anything on the Internet. To "google" someone or something, you can use Google or any other search engine. Even when using a competitor's product, most people say, "Google it." The generic use of the word "google" spread, in much the same way that "Xerox®" became an interchangeable verb for "copy."

Google technologies are tools that are simple, ubiquitous, and flexible. These three points really describe *all* Google products. The company works hard to make sure that every one of their products is easy to use, available on as many platforms and in as many places as possible, and flexible enough to meet everyone's needs. Wow...just imagine if everything in your life met those criteria!

I apply this same freedom to the word *GOOGLE'LIZE*. The verb *GOOGLE'LIZE* signifies the application of these three principles and other aspects of technology and life. There are many products created by people outside Google that also fit these guiding Google principles. Any technology that is simple, ubiquitous, and flexible could be classified as a "Google" technology in the broadest sense of the word. These technologies work together to help you *GOOGLE'LIZE Your Life*, and as you'll learn, *Google'lizing* your life means greater productivity.

Productivity = Free Time

Ultimately, this is a book about teaching you how to be productive and get more done with the precious time that you have. That being said, it's *not* about getting more done simply for the sake of doing more. I believe our goal, like Google's, should be to simplify so we can focus on what's most important to each of us.

For me, sometimes that's a side project like writing a book. But more often than not, it's spending time with my family. Because after all, it really doesn't matter how much you are getting done, if you're not doing the right things.

Book Overview

In the spirit of this simplicity, this book is divided into four major parts. Read it straight through, or jump to the sections that interest you most; your choice. While this book is not meant as a technology how-to book, I've thrown in tech tips throughout the book to get you up to speed and give you some specific steps to apply in your life.

In the first section, I focus on some general principles behind the Google Productivity System. What exactly is the role of technology? What are some general guiding principles to follow when trying to be productive? How can you visualize the process?

In the second section, I focus on the three most important Google tools to help you be productive: GoogleTasks, Gmail, and Google Calendar.

In the third part, I briefly introduce you to other technologies, both from Google, and other sources. I also jump into mobile devices and the role they play in our increasingly mobile world.

> *"The KEY to getting things done is knowing what to leave undone."*

In the final section I give you some "getting started guides" by going through the workflow of a typical day. This is where the rubber meets the road and I help you *GOOGLE'LIZE Your Life* to get more done!

Warning: applying a new system takes time. It's easy, but it won't happen simply by agreeing with the theory and wishing it to happen. I have made this book short on purpose so you can read it on one setting in just a few hours, without having to put aside days to figure it out. Just take one tip at a time; work on that and, after a day or so, employ another tip. Every little bit helps.

Part 1: Technology and Productivity

Chapter 1: Role of Technology

Computers Simplify Your Work and Enrich your Life – Really?

In 1991, there was a classic commercial from one of the first consumer computer companies. In that commercial, the announcer introduced the audience to the power of modern desktop computing. At one point, he explained that with the Internet, you can "turn your computer into a limitless source of information and resources that will *simplify your work and enrich your life.*"[1]

It has become the ultimate irony that something that was marketed to make our lives simple now makes them so complex. The idea of overcoming computer addiction, like nicotine addiction, is funny, and at the same time, scary. Know anyone who wastes hours a day on social media? Maybe it's you...? Computer addiction really isn't a joke.

Today, computers bring information into our lives at staggering rates. In fact, it's now to the degree that computers no longer help you, but hinder your productivity. I doubt you'll disagree.

There are distractions popping up constantly: You get a new e-mail, there are Web pages begging to be explored, and work just waiting to be, well postponed, right? It's no wonder that we all feel overwhelmed...all the time. We're spending all of our time trying to process all of that information and not enough time doing.

However, it's not the computer's fault. After all, they're just doing exactly what we program them to do. They're simply tools, like hammers. If you hit your thumb with your hammer, it's not the hammers fault, right? (Although invariably, we blame the hammer, not our lack of carpentry skills.)

---

[1] Emphasis added. This video can be viewed online here:
http://www.youtube.com/watch?v=0kf1DBg5vJs – Accessed 1 November 2009.

The same thing's true when using technology. The problem stems from the fact that we haven't taken the time to learn how to manage the computer. We have become slaves to the very machines that were created to make our lives simpler because we do not educate ourselves.

Well, no more...

Personal experiences help me understand theories and ideas. I also see myself so clearly in so many of the people I have the privilege of associating with each day. For that reason, I'd like to introduce you to a few fictional characters throughout this book that help clarify my points. They are combinations of people we all know and may even be ourselves at times. Let's start with Robert and Bob.

Robert – The Traditional Factory Worker

Meet Robert L. Copenhauer. Robert is perhaps, the one character that we won't be able to relate to very well, if at all. Robert lived in the early 1900's in Detroit, Michigan. Like everyone else in Robert's town, he got up every day and went to work at the factory. He sat in approximately the same spot for eight hours, and hour after hour, he added a small switch to the doors on the first Model Ts. That was his job. That was his only job. It was the classic assembly line of the industrial age, and it was cutting-edge at the time.

Despite the repetitive nature of Robert's job, he was constantly trying to find ways to be more productive...ways to install those switches faster and more efficiently.

Bob – The Modern Day Factory Worker

Here we are a century later, and Robert's great-grandson, Robert T. Copenhauer IV, whom everyone at work calls Bob, works in the same factory as his great-grandfather. Things are similar, but at the same time, they are also very different. Bob still gets up, goes to work and sits in approximately the same place all day.   But he has far from one job.   In fact, he has HUNDREDS of things he has to manage.

Bob has to monitor the machines. He has to send daily e-mail reports to his supervisor.   He has to sift through dozens of e-mails from superiors, colleagues, and employees. He has to plan, attend, and present at meetings. He has to work on his professional development.   Bob's like his great-grandfather; he's always looking for ways to be more productive, but often gets distracted by all there is to do.

Knowledge Workers

You're probably like Bob. You may have one primary job for which you're responsible, but more than likely it's just one of many, *many* secondary jobs and responsibilities. Many of us are part of a new breed of workers called knowledge workers.   Simply put, we're people who are paid for the knowledge that we have. Many of us spend a great deal of time on the computer. Many of us also spend a lot of time in meetings, or even traveling and still need access to the work and personal information on the computer.

Oh, and did I also mention that we might actually have a personal life with family and friends we care about?   We do, and they can't be neglected either. Unfortunately, all too often, they're the ones who fall by the wayside when we do a poor job of managing the work-related requests and let the influx of constantly streaming information waste our time.

Needless to say, it gets overwhelming sometimes. I'm certain you agree...probably because of first-hand experience.

The goal of this book is to bring you back to a simpler time – to make computers your assistants, to re-establish computers as subservient to man and not the other way around.

Later on, you'll also meet Ted and Sue. Both are knowledge workers who have to cope with technology in their attempts to be productive...with varying degrees of success!

Productivity Systems

A productivity system is any type of system you use to organize your life. It can be as simple as a pen and paper or as complex as six devices that sync up to one server that you can access from everywhere, all the time.

It's also important to clarify that digital productivity systems can be as simple as a text file on your desktop. They don't have to be digital PDA devices or Google systems that run in the cloud. I just so happen to think those are the best.

Paper vs. Digital

There have been mountains of books and blog posts arguing for and against paper and digital based productivity systems. Every day there are hundreds of paper and digital disciples who go head-to-head in this great productivity war. Feelings are often hurt, but there are points to be made on both sides. Here are some quick snapshots summarizing the common pros and cons of both the paper and digital productivity systems.

Paper Productivity Systems

Pros	Cons
<ul><li>Will always start</li><li>Never have to recharge</li><li>Free Form – You can write tasks in any order and easily reorder them.</li></ul>	<ul><li>No backup</li><li>One source, one point of failure</li><li>Manual repeating events</li><li>Cost of buying new calendars each year</li></ul>

One personal story: Remember my grandpa's awesome new digital PDA that got me started? Well, I also remember the day he told me he had lost all the information he had so painstakingly entered. This was "back in the day" before they thought about exporting and backing up data. Puting information into devices that could hold SO much was cool by itself! Who needed backups? But just like that, all of Grandpa's data was gone, really gone. This never happened with my plain ol' paper calendar. Well, at least not unless I lost it. Luckily backups are a whole lot better nowadays. More often than not, I have many copies of my data in many places.

Digital Productivity Systems

Pros	Cons
<ul><li>Sync with multiple sources</li><li>Backup</li><li>Repeating Events</li><li>Automated Tasks</li><li>Easy Sharing and Collaboration</li></ul>	<ul><li>Energy Dependent</li><li>Technology...need I say more?</li><li>Cost (Device)</li><li>Dependent on Programs</li></ul>

Each of these points carries different value for each person. Someone might be able to get along fine with copying his or her tasks over to a new list each day or once a week. Others just cannot bring themselves to pay for the new shiny gadget (and often the accompanying monthly plan). You must decide for yourself what's most important to you.

The beauty of the *Google Productivity System* is that you can probably use it with whatever devices you already have or just use it with your everyday desktop computer. There is no monetary investment necessary, and I like that.

Role of Technology

I'm not a big fan of technology for technology's sake or because it's trendy. There are some things that technology is going to be good for, and there are times when paper and pencil are still better. The key is knowing when to use which one. Here's how technology fares:

Technology is useful:

- For accessing information in multiple locations, in multiple formats.
- For sharing information with others.
- For simplifying and automating tasks.

Technology is not useful:

- When it takes longer to learn and use than it would without the technology. That does not take into account some of the initial time investment necessary to learn anything new.
- When it's next to impossible to learn.

Google Productivity System

The *Google Productivity System*, or *gProductivity* for short, combines all of the good things about technology. It's using Google products and other tools that follow the same "simple, ubiquitous, and flexible" mantra to be productive. It's easy to learn; it has a ton of automation and sharing built in; and Google along with other *GOOGLE'LIZE* tool companies are constantly improving it to make it better.

The Google Productivity System has three main components: Google Tasks, Gmail, and Google Calendar.

Google Tasks HUB: this is where it all happens! Your goal is to put all your *important* stuff in here.

Gmail: all-in-one mail client. Send everything here; it's your one place for e-mail communication.

Google Calendar: manage your schedule.

In addition to these three main tools that you use on a daily basis, there are other tools you might use occasionally to augment and speed up your work depending on the task at hand, which we will discuss in this book.

- Google Reader
- Flash Readers
- Google Voice
- Google Docs (Docs, Spreadsheets, Presentations, Forms, Drawings)
- Google Wave

Why Google?

I recommend using Google products in conjunction with one another since they're designed to work in sync, but you can apply this method just as well to a paper-based organization method or another software system like Outlook®, or Thunderbird®.

You can get parts of the system with other clients, but not the whole system. I've tried hundreds of programs, paper based systems, and other productivity systems. In the end, I've come to this conclusion; it simply all works better, faster, and easier using Google tools.

Too many startup companies have great plans and a great product, but they cannot sustain a free model like Google and start charging or disappear completely. Google, on the other hand, is not going away any time soon.

Google is also constantly adding new features. Chances are that by the time you read this, there will have introduced more features that make this system even more appealing. You can keep up with the latest features at our website: http://googlelize.com. You will find a link there to forums, as well as a blog where our team writes about other Google and productivity news.

Chapter 2: The Theory behind the Process

Hopefully, your eyes didn't glaze over when you read the title of this chapter. Here's the alternate title:

"Theory is boring, but for most of us, it's important to understand why we do things in order to be motivated to actually do them."

As I teach workshops and give presentations around the world on *GOOGLE'LIZING Your Life,* theory is always one of the things that people appreciate the most. It provides a base for their personal productivity and the principles we will discuss throughout this book.

Unless you understand the process, you're not going to implement it. If you don't implement it, you continue to let technology control your time rather than the other way around. It's the case of the tail wagging the dog.

Productivity Systems

The *gProductivity* system is built on the shoulders of giants. There have been many different productivity books and systems over the years, and rather than ignore these as if they didn't exist, I would like to build on them instead. Like my foray into paper calendars and Grandpa's early electronic organizer, you've probably tried more than one of these systems as well. *GOOGLE'LIZE Your Life* combines three systems into one.

Many productivity systems fail to address the role of technology. They assume we can figure it out, or that it's not important. Well, it certainly is VERY important. There are very few people who are not inundated with technology and information today, especially when it comes to knowledge workers like Bob. So we have to figure out how to manage all of it. *GOOGLE'LIZE Your Life* takes bits and pieces of these systems and puts them all together with our own technology sauce so you can use a system in which technology becomes your advocate. That's what technology was created for.

When you *GOOGLE'LIZE Your Life,* you don't have to spend hours and hours trying to shoehorn a system into the technology that is already part of your life.

First Things First

The first book is Steven Covey's *First Things First* . This book is classic. It was first published in 1994 before computers, email and the internet was even really in the picture for most of us. Covey introduces three types of productivity people.

The first are task-driven people. These are people who make lists of things to do and work off of their lists. There's a lot of satisfaction in making lists and marking things off of lists. The problem is that people who make lists of things to do will often only do things if they're on the list and leave little or no room for reflection on what's important. In our modern information society, there are also way too many things on our task lists, and they become overwhelming.

The second type of productivity people Covey introduces are the calendar-driven people. These are folks who schedule everything into their calendars. This was me when I was a little kid. I would put things in the calendar like "walk to school" and "sleep." (Hey, I already admitted I was geeky!) The big danger in this type of system is that you spend all your time organizing your system by putting entries in your calendar. And then what happens if someone walks into your office? All of 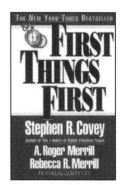 the sudden your schedule is ruined and you spend the next half hour rescheduling your day instead of being productive.

The third type of productivity people are values-driven people. These are people who work on what is *most important.* They make immediate judgments on everything they do. If it is important it goes onto their list of things to do. If the information comes up short on their values test it is simply discarded.

Some people would argue that *GOOGLE'LIZE Your Life* is actually a task-driven system because it focuses on using Google Tasks and having task lists, but I argue that it's a values-based system because the first thing you need to do when something crosses your desk is to make a values judgment on that information, task, event, etc., and then organize your task list and act according to that evaluation. You then work based on your values, and what is most important to you, and not what is on your task list.

Covey's Four Quadrants

In Steven Covey's *First Things First,* he introduces the four quadrants of urgency and importance as a method for filtering everything that's coming at us and deciding what to work on.

	Urgent	Not Urgent
Important	Crying baby Kitchen fire Some calls 1	Exercise Vocation Planning 2
Not Important	3 Interruptions Distractions Other calls	4 Trivia Busy work Time wasters

Image from Wikipedia: http://en.wikipedia.org/wiki/First_Things_First_(book)

The first quadrant on the top left contains the urgent/important things. These are things that are going to happen no matter what. If the house is on fire, you will take care of it. When the baby is crying, you have to take care of her.

The second quadrant on the top right consists of the not urgent, but important things. The classic example – exercise. No one is telling us we need to do it, so often we just neglect it. Nonetheless, it's important.

The third quadrant contains the urgent, but not important things that constantly come at us. People walking through our door, phone calls, and other distractions fall in this area. They are urgent because people or things are trying to get our attention, but in the end they are really not that important.

The last quadrant consists of the not important and not urgent quadrant. Things like TV watching at the end of the day, the reorganizing the calendar, and playing games fall into this quadrant.

Which quadrant do you spend most of your time in? If you're like me and 90% of the rest of the world, you spend most of your time in the third and fourth quadrants putting out fires here and there, and just trying to pass time till the weekend.

Modern Quadrants

I'd like to adapt Covey's four quadrants to technology and the world in which today's 21st century knowledge workers live. In which quadrant do you think that e-mail shows up? Yup, you guessed it: Most of the time it's in the urgent, but not important quadrant #3. Granted, sometimes there are important things in e-mail, but more often than not those things should be communicated via telephone anyway. We'll talk more about that in the e-mail chapter.

Remember that really urgent and important things are things that will get taken care of no matter what. If your computer crashes, the server crashes, or if there is a real fire you will take care of these things. Too often, we think something is really urgent and important, but in reality it can wait.

And the fourth quadrant is filled with things like Facebook®, YouTube®, Twitter®, and Hulu®. There are millions of virtual places where you can waste away your day, all in the name of entertainment.

The modern Covey quadrant looks something like this:

	Urgent	Not Urgent
Important	Computer Crash Some calls Real Fire! 1	Task List Exercise Review/Organize 2
Not Important	3 Email Phone Calls Interruptions	4 Facebook Twitter YouTube

You'll notice that I put our task list in the not urgent, but important quadrant #2.

Our Personal 2nd Quadrant

There is one last question that's important to me that I'd like to bring up. What items fall into your personal second quadrant? What's important to you, but you just can't seem to find the time to do because there is so much going on in the other quadrants? Spend time with family? Work on that side project? Your hobbies?

For me, my family falls into the not urgent but very important second quadrant.

That really put's it into perspective.

If I'm letting the other quadrants run my life, I won't have the time I would like to spend with my family. On the other hand, if I manage my time wisely, I will be able to spend time with them and so much more. This is the reason for everything I'm teaching here.

Each of us has our own items in the second quadrant that are important. Sometimes they're dictated by others, like our boss, but they're still important. Getting those things done is a matter of managing the rest of the quadrants, and if done right, technology can help you do that.

Covey's quadrants provide the "why" in the *GOOGLE'LIZE Your Life* system. This is the reason for all that we are doing. It's based on our personal values and what's important to us. This "why" should be incorporated into every tool and process, and without it we are simply working. It's about doing the right things, so we can focus on the most important things.

Getting Things Done

The second book I would like to briefly mention is David Allen's *Getting Things Done* (GTD). Published in 2001, Allen introduces a system is to get the unimportant things out of your mind, so you can focus on what needs to be done in the moment.

There are fundamental steps for GTD productivity:

- Collect
- Process
- Organize
- Review
- Do

"One thing you can't recycle is wasted time."

Allen jumps into the information age with his book and really gives some solid points for managing all information coming at us. Allen's first point about collecting all your information into one place is the foundation for the Google Tasks Hub. Google Tasks is your home for everything you need to do and we will get into this more in chapter three. Allen's next three points: process information, organize the things you need to get done, and reviewing those tasks are essential in any modern information age productivity system. These points will come up again and again throughout this book.

Many people criticize the GTD method because of its limited focus on actually getting things done, or 'doing'. We spend all of our time organizing our task lists and not enough time focusing on actually getting things done. This can be especially troublesome when using technology to manage your life. You have to find a system that is intuitive and easy to manipulate. Otherwise the tail's wagging the dog again.

4-Hour Workweek

The last book that I'll mention is Timothy Ferriss' *4-Hour Workweek*, published in 2007. At its core, this book is about employment, and ultimately freeing yourself from your regular job, it includes a section about specifically managing technology. In this section he does a really good job talking about reducing the information overload,

managing expectations from others, and freeing yourself from the power of technology through automation.

GOOGLE'LIZE Mantra

You can reduce the information coming in through automation and preventative measures (Ferriss). You quickly process information that comes at you based on your values (Covey) and put it into your Hub (Allen). Your Hub then becomes the center of your productivity by reviewing and organizing it regularly (Allen). You use technology to make your hub accessible in many locations, and easily organize it so you can focus on doing! All of these parts combine to create a simple, easy, and fast system for finding the things that are most important for you, and focusing on them.

The driving motto for *GOOGLE'LIZING Your Life* is really simple – *save brain cycles*. I am defining brain cycles as anything that requires you to think. This could be a simple as reading a subject line for an e-mail, or as complex as writing a report. Everything we do requires brain cycles. Although our amazing minds seem to have infinite capacity, there's only so much information you can process in any given day, and especially at any given time.

I do not believe that you can multitask and really be productive. Yes, you might be able to do multiple things, but not well. Why not just get whatever you're working on done so you can focus on more important things?

With the massive amounts of information coming at you through e-mail, conversations, and other media, you've got to figure out ways to minimize the static, so you can focus on what's most important to you. Even if you didn't need to save brain cycles, there's still that same ol' bottleneck we all face – time. You'll never get more than 24 hours per day. Saving brain cycles and controlling your time so you can focus on what is most important is really what productivity is all about.

You can reduce the amount of brain cycles you use by making sure you process all information only once, or twice at most. You shouldn't be reading and making the same decisions repeatedly. It wastes brain cycles that you can be using to do other things... more important things.

It is also important to minimize the distractions. Every time you get interrupted, for whatever reason, it takes time – precious time – and brain cycles to get back on track.

So that is the theory behind the process. Let's jump into the different components of the *GOOGLE'LIZE Your Life* system!

Part 2: Using the Tools to *GOOGLE'LIZE Your Life*...and That Means Simplifying It!

Chapter 3: Setting up your hub in Google Tasks

Time's a'wastin', so let's get started with building your own personal productivity system by exploring your hub. Your hub is where everything happens. It's where you organize your life on a daily basis. It's also where you look to try to figure out what you need to be doing next.

Think of your hub as the central gear. No matter how many other gears are added, you control the whole works when you control the central gear – your hub.

Over the years, my personal hub has taken on several different forms. I've tried everything from paper tasks systems, to e-mail clients, to mobile productivity systems, and finally to the current and best implementation with Google Tasks. Although I recommend you use Google Tasks as your hub, you can also use your e-mail client using folders, other task management software (like Outlook®, Lightning for Thunderbird®, Remember the Milk®, Toodledo®) or even a good, old-fashioned moleskin notebook.

Whatever you decide to use, there are four *essential* things to consider when figuring out what's best for your hub. You'll quickly see why Google tools are your best option for productivity.

#1 — Free-form

I've found one of the biggest hindrances to productivity is the time spent simply organizing – getting everything where you need it to be. Too many systems require excessive amounts of time to move things from one list to another, or they contain so many unneeded options that they become overwhelming.

A free-form system means that your tasks can be easily reordered and moved to different lists. The classic example of this is paper. With paper, you can easily reorder and decide what's most important and what's next without having to change 17 different properties for that task. Without a free-form system, your "doing" time is spent on the organization itself. Is this sustainable? Not a chance. Remember, the goal is for you to get productive things done, not waste time on the productivity system.

#2 — Integration with e-mail

So you may ask, if it's easiest, why don't we just use paper to organize ourselves? Here's the simple answer: When's the last time you went 24 hours without e-mail or any sort of technology? Oh, right...technology. Many of us also spend the majority of our day using our computers. While there are some people who rarely use technology, that number shrinks exponentially each day.

The majority of our communication occurs in e-mail. That leads to my second point: Because so much important information is shared in communication, your hub must integrate closely with e-mail. This will help you avoid constantly rewriting and copying tasks into your system. It also creates a reference point that can be easily retrieved and responded to when working on a task.

This is the one advantage that Google Tasks currently has over other online task systems that might have more features. It is one of only a few systems that fully integrates with e-mail at this time. You can add e-mails directly to your task list with a shortcut and keep the reference to the e-mail, so when you go to work on the task you can simply click the hyperlink for the related e-mail and open it again. Other systems like Outlook®, Thunderbird®, and Remember the Milk® have this function, but they don't have the free-form discussed above.

#3 — Multiple Lists (Categories)

Another common pitfall for task management is using only a single list. People are then overwhelmed by the sheer number of things there are to do. Combine that with too many options, and you'll give up on your task management after a week or two. Whatever you choose for your hub, it should have the ability to separate your tasks into multiple lists. I'll address how to efficiently manage multiple lists in the next section.

#4 — Easy Access

More than ever, it's important that you have access to your list of things you need to do no matter where you are. It's also important that your list is where ever you happen to be. That way, when you have an idea or remember something that needs to be done, you can easily and quickly insert it into your hub. This includes your mobile devices. You can really get some work done on those things nowadays.

Other Considerations

There are also a couple of things that may be important to consider for you and your productivity systems.

Depending on the type of work you do, you may need to collaborate online – sharing your tasks with others to show what you've done or to review the tasks assigned to others. There are a few systems out there that achieve this. The most common is Microsoft Exchange®, and an online alternative is Remember the Milk®.

Google Tasks gives the ability to share your tasks via e-mail when needed. I've heard of many people who often use this feature to show their bosses what they've done during the day.

I prefer not to share my tasks because I don't want things showing up on my task list that are not important to me. I would like to make a personal value judgment before adding it to my task list. Otherwise, it becomes a constantly growing task list. And that's exactly what we do not want.

Repeating Events

Depending on the type of work you do, your tasks may repeat on a regular basis or be ongoing. I used to think that this was really important and would put all types of events into my hub. However, I soon found that the euphoria of a new system wore off and the repeating tasks would pile up. The next thing I knew, I was giving up on my productivity system. My hub was overloaded which overloaded my brain and sent my stress level up. At a glance, it looked too chaotic... exactly the opposite effect of what I wanted in a productivity system. I find it works far better to put repeating tasks into a calendar as reminders which we will discuss in more detail in the calendar chapter.

Admittedly, for some people, Google Tasks' inability to handle repeating tasks is one of the major missing features. If you find that to be the case for you, take comfort in the fact that Google is constantly innovating and adding new features to all of their products, and it probably won't be long until they add this feature as well. I'll certainly be providing up-to-date information about this at http://googlelize.com.

Due Dates

Many organizations have strict guidelines for project completion dates, aka, the dreaded deadlines. If you're always facing deadlines and losing sleep over missing them, then you'll be pleased to know that Google Tasks integrates closely with your calendar to show your due dates and can also be organized by them. Google Calendar also allows you to easily move tasks from one day to the next by simply clicking and dragging.

Despite the ease with which due dates are presented and managed, I've found that adding due dates is more often than not a waste of time. You can easily spend more time changing and organizing your due dates than actually getting the work done. Oops, the tail's wagging the dog again, poor dog.

Your inbox should not be your hub!

I only have one rule regarding what your hub should *not* be, and that is: It should not be your inbox. (More about e-mail policies coming up in the next chapter.) For now, I'll simply re-state that your hub *should not be your inbox*. You don't want a hub that is constantly growing and filled with interruptions, which is exactly what your inbox is. If your inbox is your hub, you are living your life in Covey's second quadrant (important but not urgent) where you can't get any work done.

Remember the gear depiction of your hub? You've got to maintain control of that center gear (your hub) in order to maintain control of everything else that connects to it. Your inbox actually works like another gear adjacent to the hub. If your inbox gear takes control, it can cause all the other gears (your hub included) to spin too fast, spin backwards, or simply fly off on their own. Nothing productive about that now, is there? And who knows what injury might be sustained from all those flying gears, not to mention the hassle of putting it all back together again!

How To Organize

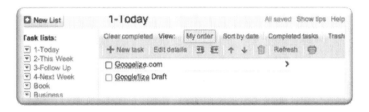

The real power of the hub is in the way that you use it. Remember – the goal is to simplify. Make organizing what you need to do easier, so that you can focus on getting work done, or more importantly, getting work done efficiently so you have time for the other important things in your life. To best do that, I find it easiest to divide my tasks up into multiple lists. These lists have three main purposes:

#1 — Timeframe Lists

Timeframe lists are the most important of the lists. These lists include 'Today', 'This Week (Soon)', and 'Next Week'. You'll notice that there are only three timeframe lists. Remember, simplicity rules, so three lists are really all you need. These timeframe lists help you focus on what's most important to do next, and here's where you put the urgent tasks and things that are important according to your own values.

#2 — Area Lists

Area lists are task lists broken up into the most important areas of your life. I have three running areas lists: Work, Home, and Websites. These are the three biggest areas where I do the most work. I will also occasionally create a special area list for large products like writing this book.

These lists serve as a repository for all the things I'd like to get done long-term. This is my "someday" storage.

#3 — Special Lists

Occasionally I will also use a special, third type of list. These lists are checklist-type lists that I use primarily for short or temporary items like shopping, trips, and other events. I always keep a shopping list to quickly jot down items I need so that I don't have to think about them until I go to the store. No brain cycles are wasted trying to remember what I need. I put it on the list and let my brain cycles focus on more important things that I need to accomplish.

Combinations

I gain maximum productivity by using the combination of all these lists. My area lists serve as my long-term storage and goals, and my timeframe lists help me focus on what's most important and needs to get done next without being distracted by everything else on my list. Again, this gives my brain cycles freedom to concentrate on getting more done, so I can focus on what's important to me. An example list might look like this:

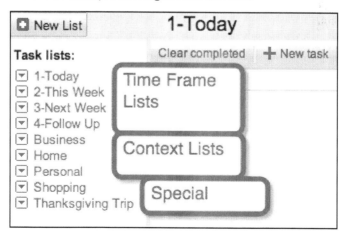

Other Task Clients

This system can easily be replicated in other task clients like Outlook®, Thunderbird®, Toodledo®, and RememberTheMilk®. Just create your category lists there. The one downside to most of these clients is that you don't have the free-form reordering ability or the ability to link to e-mail that Google Tasks has.

Workflow

So, how does this all work? I'm glad you asked! Remember in the introductory chapter we talked about organizing and processing your data quickly and saving brain cycles? This becomes especially important as we think about task management.

Process Tasks

As you process the items to put on your task lists (many of which may arrive via e-mail), you always need to think about your values and what's important to you. Make **quick** judgments and put items either onto a "Today," "This Week," or one of your long-term area lists. I've noticed over time that many of the things that I put onto my longer-term lists are not as important later on as they were when they went on to those lists in the first place. Remember, if there's a question about whether it should go on to your list, it probably shouldn't. If you're on the fence and put a task on your list, you'll have to spend time in the future assessing its importance again. Save yourself some brain cycles and avoid reading that task item again and again. Just don't put it on the list to begin with.

> "Productivity is never an accident. It is always the result of a commitment to excellence, intelligent planning, and focused effort." – Paul J. Meyer

Organize

Step 1: Once a week – no more than 15 minutes

Now that you have a list of things that you *do* need to get done, you need to start thinking about how to best organize that information. Here's my approach, and I think it will work for you too: Once a week, usually on Mondays, I look at my long-term area lists. The first thing I do is quickly prioritize from these lists what is most important right now. This is where the free-form capabilities of Google Tasks make it the best choice for task management. After I prioritize what's most important on my area lists, I move two or three things off those lists and put them onto my "This Week/Soon" list.

Step 2: Daily

The real organization takes place at the end of the day in preparation for the next day. At 4:45 every day, I sit down and review the tasks I've completed that day and the ones I'd like to accomplish the next day. This not only assists me in my organization, but also motivates me and prepares me for the next day and helps me focus on my second quadrant items like spending time with family, working out, etc. I then move tasks from my "This Week" list onto my "Today" list based on my values and what's most important to me.

Again, the purpose of multiple timeframe lists is to minimize the number of tasks you see at any one time. Don't look at your area task list on a daily basis. You already made value judgments based on what's most important to you. Focus on that first, and if you get that done, then feel free to get some more tasks from your area task lists.

"If you want to make good use of your time, you've got to know what's most important and then give it all you've got." – Lee Iacocca

When I come in to work the next day, I will not open my e-mail. I look at my "Today" list, and *only* my "Today" list, and start working on the tasks that I have ahead of me for the day.

Keyboard Shortcuts

Every program has keyboard shortcuts, but most people don't take the time to learn them. TAKE THE TIME! You may be thinking that using your mouse only takes an extra two seconds each time. Two seconds is nothing, right? Wrong. If you use your mouse two hundred times a day (admittedly a conservative estimate), those measly two seconds turn into almost thirty hours over the course of the year. Thirty hours! Why you could almost take a full week's worth of vacation, if you'd just learn the shortcuts. Maybe you can convince your boss to give you some extra vacation time if you learn the shortcuts. Okay, maybe not, but you get the picture, and two seconds becomes thirty hours, a lot of time that you can dedicate to what's important to you.

Keyboard shortcuts save you from moving your mouse around and clicking on different things. Over time our fingers learn what's important, and using keyboard shortcuts becomes rote motor memorization. Do you use "control/command c" to copy and "control/command v" to paste? I'm guessing that you do. You took the time to learn that and use it to save time.

Google tasks has some great shortcuts for quickly navigating around inside of your tasks.

Cmd/Ctrl up and down arrow	Reorder tasks
Tab, Shift-Tab	Indent and out-dent tasks to create a hierarchy.
Shift-Enter	Edit task details, including due dates or notes.
Esc	Close Tasks

The danger with this system, just like any other, is spending too much time organizing. I really try to minimize the distractions by using multiple lists, but again, it must be simple. Simplicity is the key – they key to all happiness, peace of mind and productivity. Don't create too many lists, and don't have too many things on your lists. This gives you the greatest chance to focus on getting the most important things done and helps you minimize the distractions. Keep it simple; get it done.

"Today at work, I received 650 E-mails from feedme@homecat.com! Was that you?"

Meet Sue. Sue has worked at the same company for the past 17 years as an administrative assistant. When she started working there, the company didn't even have e-mail. When she started, her responsibilities were to type letters and manage clients for the boss. Over the years, she moved up the ranks, and her job changed dramatically. Somewhere along the way, she got e-mail and started to keep track of her life online. She half-heartedly tried several different organizational methods using folders, but those never seemed to work for her. She spent too much time organizing and not enough time doing.

One thing Sue never did was delete e-mail, and today she has 17,456 e-mails in her inbox. She also has 78 different folders and sub folders, none of which she really uses. When Sue needs something, she searches for it in her inbox, or tries to remember the folder she stuck it in, but she is constantly forgetting assignments. Her e-mails don't serve as reminders. But even more importantly, Sue feels completely overwhelmed every time she looks at her e-mail. She can sometimes spend hours trolling her inbox reading through old items to find what she needs   Sue is not alone either; millions of us were never taught how to manage e-mail. It appeared on our desktops, and we were told to use it. This book is intended to help those who, like Sue, feel overwhelmed by e-mail. Maybe the idea of never having e-mail is foreign to you. Either way, here are a couple of tips on being a little more productive with this constant source of interruption.

Choosing the Right Client – Why I Use Gmail

There are dozens and dozens of e-mail clients (an e-mail client is the term for computer program used to manage e-mail) out there (Thunderbird®, Outlook®, Mac Mail® etc.), as well as hundreds of online mail programs (Gmail, Hotmail®, Yahoo®, or your Internet service provider). So how do you know which e-mail client to use? I have four characteristics you should look for in an e-mail client that will help you be more productive.

#1 – Multiple E-mail Accounts

Send mail from another address

When receiving a message:
◉ Reply from the same address the
○ Always reply from default address

Today, almost everybody has multiple e-mail addresses. Some people suggest that you keep separate e-mail inboxes for your work and personal life. On the other hand, I suggest that you put all of your e-mail addresses into one e-mail client. Remember that our goal is to save brain cycles. More inboxes require more brain cycles.

Many e-mail clients allow you to add multiple accounts and send as if you are sending from those specific accounts. This is one of the lesser-known features of Gmail and one that makes it a good solution for many people. It allows you to add your work e-mail address, your personal e-mail address, your business address, and as many other addresses as you want. You can then send from each of those addresses from within one e-mail inbox.

To add another e-mail address to your Gmail account, simply click **Settings – Accounts and Import** and click the "Send mail from another address" button and follow the prompts.

#2 – Threaded Conversations

E-mail has become such an important part of communication that often times we'll carry on entire conversations via e-mail. This results in dozens of e-mails in your inbox for a single conversation. Gmail has a fantastic feature that groups all these e-mail conversations into one e-mail making your inbox less cluttered and your brain less overwhelmed. It also makes it easier to find information again in the future.

Other e-mail clients (like Thunderbird® and Outlook®) offer similar add-ons and configurations that allow you to achieve the same result.

#3 – Search vs. Tagging e-mails vs. Folders

One of the questions that people in my productivity classes ask is: "How do we find information again easily?" Because we spend so much time on e-mail, it becomes our filing system of sorts, and that's okay to some extent. The problem occurs when you spend excessive amounts of time filing e-mails away into folders in case you need to retrieve the information they contain in the future. Chances are good that when you need it, you won't even remember what folder you stuck it in. Wasted brain cycles, and the tail's wagging the dog again.

Modern e-mail clients are so advanced that you can often find e-mails by simply doing a search for the sender, the subject, or a phrase that you remember from the e-mail. If dear, old Sue remembers that there was information about a meeting with Bob, all she has to do is type "meeting with Bob" into her e-mail client's search box, and it narrows her search. Of course, in Sue's case, instead of searching through 17,456 e-mails, she now only has to search through 3,987 e-mails.

I used to spend a lot of time filing away e-mails as well, but I have found that that is no longer necessary and suggest that you simply put all e-mails into an archive. That means one folder where everything resides. That's right. One folder. One archive.

Gmail has a nice feature built in for archiving. After you respond to an e-mail or add it to your hub, you simply click the archive button, and it goes into an "All Mail" folder. There are even shortcuts to speed up this process even more.

If you're using another e-mail client, create one folder called "processed e-mail." After you finish with an e-mail, move it to that folder. Done. This also significantly reduces search time as the search engine doesn't have to look through multiple folders to find the e-mail you're looking for.

I've given productivity workshops all over the United States, and I often meet people who say that they simply cannot give up folders and that folders are absolutely necessary for their organization. To that I say: Everyone can adopt the system to greatly reduce the time they spend processing e-mail. Plus it saves brain cycles and gives you more time to do what's important. Filing e-mails is not important. It's a waste of your valuable time. Let technology do the work, not you.

#4 – Accessible in MANY places instantly – Web, Mobile, etc.

You'll remember from the introduction that one of the tenants of Google is to make all information accessible in as many locations as possible. This is especially important for e-mail. If you can only access your e-mail at work, you miss out on the possibility of processing e-mail on your mobile phone while you're out and about.

Everyone has also dealt with the pain of setting up a new computer and trying to get your e-mail set up the way it was before. After all, we're nothing if not creatures of habit. With Gmail and other Web-accessible e-mail clients, it's the same no matter what computer you're on, no matter where you're located, and no matter what device you're using. There's no telling the amount of time that will save you in the future.

Google has mobile e-mail clients for almost every mobile device out there. This includes Blackberries®, Windows Mobile Devices®, iPhones®, android phones, and Web-optimized versions for hundreds more. To find out more, or download Gmail for your mobile device, go to http://www.google.com/mobile/gmail/.

Prevention vs. Reaction

Ben Franklin is remembered for many famous quotes such as: "An ounce of prevention is worth a pound of cure." (Ben was a smart guy. In fact, if Ben were alive today, he'd be using Google Tasks.) Prevention is the key. When it comes to e-mail, there are things you can do to prevent messages from hitting your inbox in the first place, so you don't have to read or be interrupted by them. Then there are things you can do to quickly process the e-mail that you do read.

Prevention

Your goal should be to make sure that your inbox is as clean and empty as possible, so that when you come to process your e-mail, it doesn't become your hub. It remains simply a place of communication. You can take steps to ensure that unimportant messages don't even reach your inbox, so you can focus on responding to the e-mails that really are important when you do process e-mail. This also helps you greatly reduce the amount of time spent in your inbox in the first place, which, in turn, also reduces the chance that you might get distracted by something else while you're there. No interruptions, no wasted time, no unnecessary brain cycles. Remember any time you even have to read a message subject line, or delete a message, you are using brain cycles, or effort, that you could be using on more important things, like your family.

Current E-mail Policy

The single most important thing that you can do to manage your e-mail is to set up a policy that governs your e-mail actions. This policy has several facets; the most important of which is how often you check your e-mail. The first thing most people do when they get to work is open up their e-mail and start checking. This process can take anywhere from 15 minutes to several hours depending on what you find in your e-mail. (It takes Sue almost until lunch, as you might have guessed.)

Then, after they have finally weeded through all the messages, they minimize it and leave it open. There's the interruption kiss of death right there. Oh sure, they try to work on their task list, but before long a little notification appears that "you've got new mail" and what happens? Productivity comes to a screeching halt.

You know the drill: You stop everything else and go look at that e-mail. You might respond, or you just read the e-mail and leave it in your inbox. Either way, it takes several minutes to remember where you were and what you were working on to get back to work. You just wasted those precious cycles.

E-mail Policy

I suggest you only check your e-mail twice a day, once at 12:00 PM and once at 4:00 PM. This suggestion actually comes from Tim Ferriss' book "4-Hour Work Week". He's correct when he says that these two times are the best times to check e-mail because that gives people the most time to respond to the e-mails that you send to them. Then you can quickly process e-mail, as many at a time as you can, CLOSE your e-mail, and get back to work on your task list. If you've got doubts, did you notice the title of his book? He's on to something.

I've taught this principle in other workshops, and this is certainly the most difficult to adopt. As human beings, we crave attention and affection from the people with whom we associate. There was an article written in which e-mail was compared to the classic experiment with mice and random rewards. (E-mail: The Variable Reinforcement Machine – http://www.codinghorror.com/blog/2009/09/email-the-variable-reinforcement-machine.html.)

In the experiment, there were two sets of mice. The study was to see how often a mouse would press a button to receive food. One set of mice received their food on a regular basis – once an hour – no matter how often they pressed the lever. The second set of mice received food on a random cycle, meaning they didn't know how many times they had to hit the lever before food would come out. In the end, the mice that received food only once an hour learned that they did not need to press the lever as much, and the mice that received food at random intervals would just sit at the lever and keep pressing it again and again.

This article compared the way that people check e-mail to the mice pressing the lever at random intervals. They concluded that e-mail is an addiction because it randomly rewards people. Although we don't know what type of e-mail we might be getting, it's still a reward to us. And very often, people will just keep pressing the *"I get mail; therefore I am." – Scott Adams* "send/receive" or "check mail" button again and again, just like the mice, hoping for some sort of reward. Do you see yourself in that scenario? Checking and checking and checking your inbox for that nugget of attention?

When we limit the intervals at which we check our e-mail, we train ourselves not to be addicted to the e-mail reward and use it for what it is – a tool for communication.

Managing Expectations

I've found that limiting the number of times e-mail is checked is one of those things that people really want to try, but they aren't sure they can. Expectations are already set and must be broken. I've found that the easiest way to manage those expectations is with an auto responder that notifies people that you will only be checking e-mail twice a day, or inserting it as part of your signature. I've tried both methods and prefer the less conspicuous signature method. Besides, using an auto-responder is going to fill up your colleagues' inboxes unnecessarily. If I ever send you an e-mail or reply, you'll notice (after my traditional signature with my contact information including my mobile phone) the following blurb:

> **E-MAIL POLICY: I try to only check e-mail twice daily at 12:00PM ET and 4:00 PM ET. If you require urgent assistance, please contact me via the phone number listed above.**

Additionally, I preemptively talked with all the people I communicate with regularly and let them know about the change I was making. I make a point to share this with new clients and colleagues when we discuss exchanging e-mails on any topic.

Instant Message Policy

This seems like the appropriate place to take a moment to talk about instant messaging. IM'ing can be a fantastic tool for getting quick answers to questions, but too often in our socially challenged world, it replaces personal communication. People will start chatting with you if you're online, and you'll let them! Before you know it, you've spent 15 minutes typing to someone when you could have said the same information in three minutes by picking up the phone and talking to them. More than likely, the verbal conversation would've even been richer and built up that relationship even more. Make sure you don't abuse IM as an alternative to personal communication.

Facebook®, Gmail®, and other instant messaging platforms are usually turned on by default.

Turn chat off. If it's on, it is just another distraction waiting to happen while you're trying to get things done. Even when the chats are quick questions, it will take you a few minutes to get your train of thought back, if you can get it back at all. Either way, it just wasted some more time and brain cycles.

If your work requires that you leave your instant message client on, minimize it, and make sure you use the status capabilities to let others know when you're not available to talk so you can focus on getting things done.

E-mail Lengths

You've all received the dreaded business e-mail. You know the one. The one where John rambles on and on about his weekend and shares all sorts of personal information before getting to the point of his e-mail. You think to yourself, "What was the point of that e-mail? I just wasted five minutes of my life reading something that he could have said in two sentences."

Well, take a lesson from John. Get to the point in your e-mails. If you send long e-mails to other people, they're more likely to reply with long e-mails as well. I've actually tried to adopt that same philosophy in writing this book. I don't want to waste your time reading too many things that aren't important to you and don't improve your productivity.

Now, I need to take a moment to differentiate between *business and personal* e-mails. Remember earlier when I discussed values? I only recommend writing brief and to-the-point *business* e-mails. For me, *personal* e-mails are often the only form of communication I have with my family members and friends. This is important communication and deserves the time that I dedicate to writing and responding to those e-mails. If I write brief e-mails to my friends, chances are they'll either choose not respond or respond with little or no information that is useful to me to build relationships with them.

E-mail Not Addressed to You

Every day when Bob comes in to work and looks into his inbox, he instantly sees 10 to 12 things he can delete right away. If there are messages coming into your inbox that are not addressed directly to you, you have managed to get onto a mailing list of some type. These e-mails generally fall within three areas.

1) SPAM
2) Mail lists containing information that you **Don't Need**

3) Mail lists containing information that you **Need**

SPAM

SPAM is unwanted advertisements, usually for embarrassing things like pharmaceutical and body enhancements. There are some statistics indicating that over 90% of all e-mail is SPAM of some sort.[2] It's a huge problem. Even if all you do is just delete all your spam every day, it still takes up brain cycles that can be used for doing something else.

"Like almost everyone who uses e-mail, I receive a ton of spam every day. Much of it offers to help me get out of debt or get rich quick. It would be funny if it weren't so exciting." – Bill Gates

If you are getting SPAM in your inbox, the first thing you can do is switch to Gmail. You knew I was going to say that, didn't you? Gmail has an amazing built-in SPAM filter that automatically deletes all your SPAM without even having to train it. It uses the aggregated knowledge of all the other users who mark messages as SPAM to identify unwanted advertisements in e-mail. I've been using Gmail since its early beta stages and have only had to delete SPAM once or twice... ever. Not once or twice a day or a week or a month. I really do mean once or twice ever.

Other e-mail clients require you to train your SPAM filter to recognize what you consider SPAM. This is where cloud productivity, or email that lives on the web, wins again since you never have to train your filter or set it up again. It will be the same on all computers, all platforms, no matter where you are and automatically deletes all SPAM from your inbox.

---

[2] Lance Witney, "Report: Spam now 90 percent of all email." Published on CNet News May 26th, 2009. http://news.cnet.com/8301-1009_3-10249172-83.html

"...and you spent 5.73 years of your life deleting spam from your e-mail."

Information you Don't Need – UNSUBSCRIBE

If you're like me, over the years you've subscribed to dozens and dozens of newsletters, mailing lists, informational e-mails, motivational e-mails, quote e-mails, and much more. It's almost like a disease. You feel important because you can say that you get so many e-mails. But from now on, you'll feel important because you get so much done.

When you look at your inbox twice a day, if you instantly delete any e-mails without reading anything more than the sender or the subject, these are prime candidates for unsubscribing. You don't need that information. You're deleting without reading. Even though it only takes a few minutes to delete these e-mails, those minutes add up, and you waste time.

Gmail has recently added a new feature that actually automatically unsubscribes you from listservs that you don't want to be part of. It recognizes when e-mails come from mail lists and gives you the option to unsubscribe from the drop down menu on the right-hand side.

As those e-mails come in over the next few days take the few minutes needed to unsubscribe and save yourself from future e-mails.

Information That You Do Need - Rules and Filters

So what do you do with information from mail lists that you actually need or think that you might need at some point? Take a close look at those e-mails, and if you can justifiably determine that you *can* read them at later date, then set up rules and filters for those e-mails.

A rule automatically moves messages out of your inbox and into folders before you even see them. They can also automatically delete messages or even send automatic replies based on the message. All modern e-mail programs have these rules. In Gmail, you can click on the drop-down to the right-hand side of an e-mail. Rules are designed to respond to various parts of the message. For example, all messages from a particular sender are automatically labeled or all messages that have a certain key phrase in the subject line are labeled and then archived (this is good for mail lists). You can then view the items by clicking on the label when you need to, but you don't have to see it as part of your regular e-mail processing.

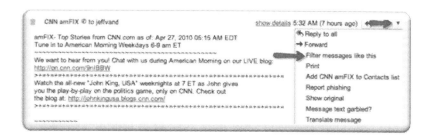

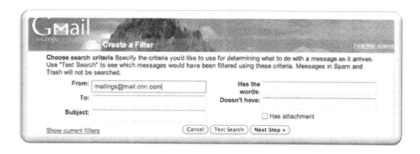

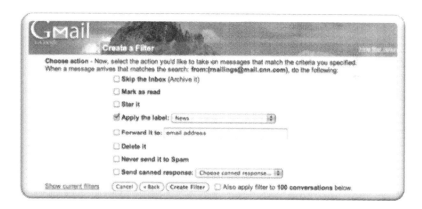

A colleague of mine actually uses rules to filter out all his bills so that he doesn't have to read them as they come in. Once a month, he goes into his bills folder and processes everything at once. His inbox is not cluttered throughout the month, and he can focus on responding to e-mails that do come in.

I've used rules to filter out all the news items that come into my inbox. I found that over the years these items are no longer important to me. Obviously when I subscribed to those mailing lists, I thought I needed the information, but in the end, it just turned out to be a distraction. You'll find that over time, setting up rules and filters forces you to be more selective about which mailing list you subscribe to.

Reactionary Measures

So, now you've managed to reduce the number of e-mails coming into your inbox, but what do you do with e-mails that are left? You've got read, process, and possibly act on them, and you'll want to do that quickly and efficiently. There are several things you do that will speed up the time it takes you to process them, and it will save those brain cycles! I call these things reactionary measures because you are reacting to the e-mail messages that come in.

Two-minute rule

The two-minute rule has probably had the most impact on my productivity since I first read about it in David Allen's *Getting Things Done* several years ago. It's a simple concept: If you can do it in two minutes or less, do it now. Got that? Two minutes or less...just get it done...NOW. David Allen applies this to all facets of life, but I'd like to apply this habit to e-mail. You'll be amazed at how many of your e-mails you can process in two minutes or less. Because e-mail is such a prevalent form of communication and many people don't know how to use it, I estimate that 80 to 90% of all e-mails can be responded to in two minutes or less.

If you cannot respond to an e-mail in two minutes or less, put it on your calendar or your task list. After that (and the next step is critical), move that message out of your inbox and into your archive, which brings us to our next point.

Inbox Zero

There's a group of productivity experts out there who swear by the concept of "Inbox Zero." This idea was introduced and made famous by Merlin Mann. The whole process can be summed up as quickly processing your e-mail into actionable items and getting out of your inbox. Every time you check your email you should leave it with zero messages when you are done. That way all your actionable items are on your task list and you can close your email out.

E-mail should not be the place where you're productive; it is simply a means of communication.

Get in, process e-mails by replying (2 minutes), putting it on your calendar or task list, and get out.

No "work" allowed here.

With Gmail, quickly processing e-mail is quite easy because you can quickly archive a message or delete it with a keystroke. Once you respond, put it on your calendar, or add it to your task list, that e-mail should be archived so that you don't think about it again until you need to address it. The task list will automatically put a link back to the e-mail no matter where it is.

I know that many of you have probably been using folders for years, but today is the day that changes. Take a deep breath – you can do it – and don't be like Sue, who by the way now has increased her inbox by another 137 messages and added seven more folders. I want to reiterate the power of search. The only folders you should have are ones to capture messages that are automatically filtered and re-directed for later reference.

The human mind doesn't follow information into folders; it remembers bits and pieces about the message, but not necessarily where it's stored. Use technology for what it does best – scanning for phrases and locations at incredible speed. Search features allow you to look up e-mails based on those ideas and those bits and pieces that your mind brings to the forefront.

Archive

When Gmail was created, they introduced the idea of an 'archive." An archive is a place where information like email is stored. Built into Gmail is an All Mail, or Archive folder where everything goes. You can recreate the same archive function in other email clients by simply creating a folder called "All Mail" and putting all your messages there after you have added them to your task list.

But I have 6327 messages in my inbox!

Let me introduce one more popular e-mail management concept: E-mail bankruptcy. If you've got thousands and thousands of messages in your inbox (or even more than you can possibly sort through and delete or add to your task list), get rid of them. Like bankruptcy, you eliminate everything and start over. I suspect our old friend, Sue, would find this impossible. But don't be like Sue; she's not very productive, busy, yes; productive, no. Bob, on the other hand, took this step and realized he immediately gained more time to get real work done. Bob's big on saving brain cycles.

Here's how you declare e-mail bankruptcy: Send a short e-mail out to all your most important contacts similar to this:

Dearest friends,

Today I am declaring e-mail bankruptcy. I'm working on improving my productivity, and rather than spending hours and hours going through all the e-mails in my inbox, I am going to put them in a folder and start from scratch. If you can resend me items that need my attention, I now have a great system in place for managing them and will be sure to respond. Thanks for understanding.

Jeff

People will appreciate your honesty and will gladly resend tasks that are important. In fact, you may find that you start a trend, and get similar bankruptcy statements from your colleagues.

Once you've done this, select all items in your inbox and drag them to your archive. In this sense email bankruptcy is more of email archiving. You still have the emails and can get to them if you need to, but you are distracted by them. People will then send you the most important things to get done and you can prioritize them in your new productivity system.

There's a nice little select all button in Gmail on the top left. If you're using a local e-mail client you select all by pressing Ctrl/Cmd A and then drag your e-mails into your archive (or delete them if you are feeling especially daring).

How to quickly process E-mails

Labels

Unfortunately, not all e-mails are created equal. Some e-mails are certainly more important than others. Gmail and other e-mail clients have the ability to tag an item with labels quickly, or change the color of the item based on the subject, the sender, or other specifications you set. This is very similar to rules mentioned above.

Some colleagues use a label to turn all e-mails that come from their bosses into a bright, red color, so they can easily see those messages and respond to those first. A word of caution about that: Not everything can be urgent, or you'll immediately defeat the system.

I also use labels to differentiate which e-mail accounts are coming into my inbox. All messages sent to my personal e-mail account have an identifying label, so I know they're probably from friends and family.

This process really helps you to see what things are important quickly, what things can wait, and what things might need to be unsubscribed or deleted.

Keyboard Shortcuts

Below is a list of the most common keyboard shortcuts I use on a regular basis in Gmail. To use them all you need to do is press these keys while in the inbox, or message.

?	Open Keyboard Shortcuts
enter	Open message
e	Archive Conversation (E-mail Message)
r	Reply
a	Reply All
f	Forward E-mail
#	Trash E-mail
g then i	Go to inbox
/	Put cursor in search box
Shift T	Add mail to Task List

I always use shortcuts to navigate my e-mail quickly. You can select an e-mail from your inbox by pressing the x key. You can also move up and down the list using the j and k keys. When I first get into my inbox, I will quickly scan the subject lines and use the j and k keys to highlight the messages I don't need. I will then hit the y key and archive those messages. I'm left with only the messages that need to be processed. Using the j and k keys, I navigate to the e-mail messages and hit the enter key to open the message. Here is a full list of keyboard shortcuts available through Gmail. You can see this list by clicking the '?' button while in Gmail with keyboard shortcuts enabled (see next page for instructions on how to enable keyboard shortcuts).

I can reply (r); I can archive (y); I can delete (Shift-#); I can add tasks (Shift-T); I can do everything required to process my e-mail without touching the mouse. You'll be amazed at the amount of time you save every day, and how quickly you can get out of your e-mail and back to focusing on your task list, back to getting things done.

When you're first getting started with keyboard shortcuts, find the most important keyboard shortcuts (the ones you might find the most helpful), print them out, and tape them up next to your monitor. You will probably look at the cheat sheet for a while, but soon you'll find that your fingers know what they need to do. Little things that matter, and these little things add up over time to save you a lot of time during the day.

By default, keyboard shortcuts are not enabled in Gmail. To enable them, simply click settings, and then look for the keyboard shortcuts area of the general tab. Click the radio button next to keyboard shortcuts to turn it on and make sure you hit 'save changes' at the bottom. You may need to refresh your screen before the keyboard shortcuts work.

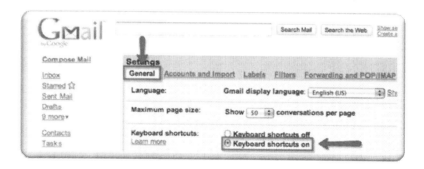

For me, the keyboard shortcuts in Gmail are better and faster than any other shortcuts I've found in other programs. This is what allows me to process e-mail quickly and one of the big reasons I use Gmail. If you cannot use Gmail, there are also shortcuts for Outlook®, Thunderbird®, and other e-mail clients. Just Google it and you'll find them. Then take the time to learn them!

Workflow

How does the actual workflow look? Remember when we talked about Stephen Covey's values and *"First Things First"* – and his four quadrants, and those that make decisions based on values, and what's most important to them? This is especially relevant when processing e-mail. You've now done all that you can to stop e-mail from entering your inbox, but from the moment you start to react to e-mail, you need to make decisions based on what's important to you.

The first thing I do when I get into my inbox is take a quick look at all the e-mails. Right away, I look to see if there's anything I can delete. It's like looking for the low hanging fruit. We're all on many mailing lists; some information we need, but some of it we don't. (Again, take a few seconds to "unsubscribe" to stale information and newsletters. While it only takes a second to delete, remove the need to delete in the future by unsubscribing in the first place. Those seconds add up!)

I see if I can garner information on the remaining messages from the subject lines and excerpts (or preview) from the e-mail that I see in my inbox. We have a policy at work that whenever someone will be out, he or she sends an e-mail to the staff listserv letting everyone else know. I don't need to waste my time reading those. I can get the information I need from the subject line. So after I read that I delete them immediately.

Next, I look at other mailing lists that come to my inbox. Remember, it's tempting to simply delete those listservs that you're not a part of, but instead take the time to open those e-mails, scroll to the bottom and unsubscribe.

This takes less than two minutes and saves you from seeing those e-mails in the inbox in the future. It saves you future brain cycles.

At this point, you'll usually have e-mails strictly addressed to you – e-mails to which you may need to respond. Start at the top, quickly read the e-mail and make a decision based on *your values* if you want to respond to it. If not, archive it or delete it. If you must respond, can you do so two minutes or less? If so, do it right then. If not, make a value judgment about when you want to respond. If it's today, add it to your "Today" list; if it's this week, add it to your "This Week" list; and if you'd like to respond someday, add it to your contacts list. Archive the e-mail, and move on to the next.

Using this method, it rarely takes me more than 15 to 20 minutes to process my entire e-mail inbox – even at times when I have 50 messages in my inbox.

Be prudent as you think about tasks and things that you might want to "one day" read or do. I've found that, over time, using this method helps to differentiate between what's important and what's not. It helps me focus on the things that need to get done and let the unimportant things fall out of my life. Every action you take and everything you do should be a reflection of what's important to you.

After you process your messages, make sure you close your e-mail until the next time you need to process again. This allows you to focus on your task list, and not be distracted or interrupted by incoming e-mails.

Getting started with Gmail

Well, this all sounds great, Jeff. But how do I get started? Moving over to Gmail is quite easy. You can create a free account by going to http://Gmail.com. Click the "create an account" button on the bottom right-hand side and follow the directions for setting up your account.

Once you set up your account and have added your business accounts, you may want to get all your old e-mails into Gmail. There are two ways to do this. If you have an online e-mail address like Yahoo®, Hotmail®, AOL®, or some other webmail program, you can easily import all your mail by going to "settings – accounts" and looking for the "import mail and contacts" button at the top. Just follow the prompts.

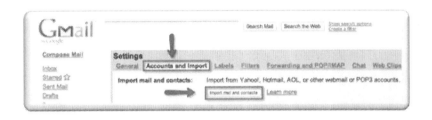

However, if you would like to move all of your exchange mail or other business mail, you can also set up Gmail within Outlook®, Thunderbird®, and other desktop mail clients. After you set up Gmail as an additional account, you can highlight all your local business e-mail and drag it all over into Gmail. Once you drag it over, you'll make a copy on the Gmail servers, and you'll be able to search your old mail for messages. Or this might be a great time to declare e-mail bankruptcy – unless, of course, you're Sue, who by the way, is now up to 17,678 e-mails.

Canned Responses – multiple signatures

I've found that I like to add different signatures to my Gmail account depending on the e-mail address from which I'm sending. The easiest way to do this is to use the canned responses feature. To enable it, select "settings – tabs" and scroll down to see the canned responses area. Click the radio button next to "enable," and click the save changes button.

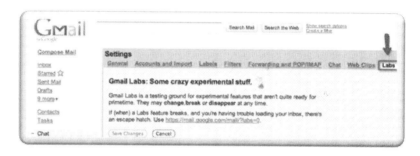

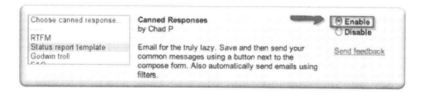

Next you need to create your canned responses. To do this, compose a regular e-mail. Type your signature in the message area as you'd like it to appear in your outgoing messages. Then click the canned responses drop-down button and select the "new canned response" option. Enter a name for your signature and hit the "okay" button. You can now safely go back to your inbox and compose a message. To use your canned response signature, click the canned response link and a drop-down menu appears. Select the signature you'd like to use.

You can also use canned responses for setting up filters to respond to people automatically, or just to save you time when you are constantly sending the same e-mails.

© Randy Glasbergen
glasbergen.com

"On Mondays, I get ready to plan my week.
On Tuesdays, I plan my week. On Wednesdays,
I revise my plan for the week. On Thursdays, I put
my plan for the week into my computer. On Fridays,
I think about starting my plan for next week."

Chapter 5: Calendar productivity

The third tool in your productivity trio is your calendar. Your calendar, like your hub, contains all your task items. Plus, your calendar contains all of your appointments for things that you need to get done. My calendar plays an important role: It helps me know when I can work on my task list and when I need to be somewhere.

In this section, I'm going to share some general tips about how you can *GOOGLE'LIZE* your calendar. Remember, *GOOGLE'LIZING* your calendar does not necessarily mean that you have to use Google; you can use the same thinking and features with any system. Many of these features can be found in all calendar programs.

In the same way that it's important for you to choose the right e-mail client, it's also important for you to choose the right calendar. And there are many good reasons to choose Google Calendar. First and possibly most importantly is that it's intuitive. Many people will recognize the layout from other calendaring systems that they've used in the past. It looks like a regular calendar, with day, week, and month views. You can create a new entry by highlighting the time for an appointment and typing in the title of the event.

Like the other components in your productivity system, your calendar solution needs to be accessible in many places instantly. You need to be able to reference your calendar on your mobile phone, at work, and at home. To really leverage your productivity, it's also important that others can be able to see your calendar and suggest times for meetings. Before we get into the technical details, let's talk about some general calendar principles.

Reserved (sacred) time

The first thing that you need to do on your calendar is reserve time for yourself. I call this my sacred time, but you can call it whatever you want. I reserve this time on my calendar for doing the things that are most important to me in the first place. This becomes especially important as you share your calendar and make it available for other people to schedule things with you. I recommend that you schedule your e-mail checking time as sacred time. Remember, you've already limited that to only twice a day. That way you won't be interrupted by others, and you'll be able to focus on actually processing your e-mail quickly.

Again, I apply the full minimalism here. Only put things on your calendar that are actually sacred to you. It might be things like working out or working on some sort of project. However, I do not recommend that you put your task list items into your calendar. People who do this often spend way too much time putting the items into the calendar and not enough time actually getting stuff done. There's that tail wagging the dog again. If you do need to set aside time to work on a specific task, just put a general entry into your calendar by creating an event and giving it the title 'hold'. Otherwise you'll spend excessive amounts of time moving things around on your calendar that you need to get done rather than simply doing them.

Repeats

Calendars are great for helping you to remember items. I don't put too many repeating items into my task list. Instead, I add them as repeating events in my calendar. When they come up, I can then make my value decision and decide to put them onto my "Today" list or ignore them completely. (Note: If you choose to ignore something, just delete it. Otherwise, you're reading it again and again throughout the day as you look at your calendar. Wasted brain cycles.)

> *"For disappearing acts, it's hard to beat what happens to the eight hours supposedly left after eight of sleep and eight of work."*
> *– Doug Larson*

Google has a fantastic repeating system: You can choose to repeat for specific time frames, repeat on certain days of the month, or even repeat based on a particular day of the week in the month.

Ticklers

A tickler is a reminder that you put in your calendar to remind you about a task that needs to happen on a certain date. This idea comes from David Allen's "Getting Things Done." If you have something that comes into your e-mail or on your task list but doesn't need thought or action until a certain day, go ahead add that as an entry into your calendar. You won't have to think about it until that day arrives. It then "tickles" your memory, and you can add it to your task list or complete the item. Good examples of this are required renewals (like magazine subscriptions) and items that have due dates (like library books).

Multiple calendars

Google and other calendar systems have the ability to create multiple calendars. This is one of those things that can be both a blessing and a curse. I recommend that you create different calendars for different areas of your life. For example, I have one for work and one for home. I also have a calendar I use for scheduling our training facility.

Each calendar shows up on the left-hand side of your screen in Google. You can add more calendars by simply clicking the "Create" button on the left-hand side underneath the list of your current calendars.

You can also give each calendar a different color by clicking the drop-down on the name next to each calendar. This helps me to get a visual overview of what my day looks like and where I'll be spending my time. Sometimes, it's actually a wake-up call because when my entire calendar is filled with dark blue – the color of my work calendar – I know I need to spend more time on green – the color of my family.

I should mention that you can show as many of these calendars simultaneously as you want, or hide them as well, with just the click of a button. On a Google Calendar, you can hide/show any calendar by simply clicking on the name of the calendar on the left hand side of your screen.

Subscriptions

Google, and other calendaring systems like Outlook® and iCal®, allow you to subscribe to calendars that have been pre-made. This saves you a tremendous amount of time since you don't have to enter items manually. I use this for subscribing to sporting events like my beloved basketball team. I subscribe once, and my calendar automatically populates, so I know when upcoming events are happening. I can keep my time free to go and cheer on the team.

To subscribe to internet calendars do a search for the topic you are interested in like "UNC-CH Basketball .ical." The .ical is the type of file needed to subscribe to calendar. Sports directories and team Web pages often will have these .ical calendars on their pages. Once you find the .ical file, just copy the URL. It will look something like http://www.unc.edu/basketball.ical. Go to your Google calendar, and at the bottom under "Other Calendars" click the "Add" button, and select the "By URL" option. Paste the URL you copied before into the field, and click the "Add Calendar" button. The calendar will then show up on the list of available calendars that you can show. It will also be updated automatically from whoever is publishing the calendar.

You can also create a calendar like this for your organization and publish the .ical URL on a webpage. Just create a new calendar, and go to the settings page to find the public .ical address.

You can also subscribe to internet calendars in other calendar programs like iCal® and Outlook® if you use them.

Sharing

Sharing is one of the most powerful features of a Google Calendar and one that I use heavily. Google Calendar has the ability to share calendar entries with anyone in the world. Not only can you share with them, you can decide exactly how much they see – ranging from only free/busy time to seeing everything you're doing.

I use this several different ways. First, I share all my calendars with my sweet wife. This allows her to see where I am immediately in case she needs to reach me. She can also add entries to my calendar. The benefits of this are easy to see. No more "I have to see if he's free." Of course, I don't always get full veto power regarding social events, but that's okay.

I also share my free/busy time on my work calendar with the world by embedding it on a webpage. This becomes extremely helpful when I'm trying to set up appointments with people or when people are trying to set appointments with me. Instead of exchanging dozens of e-mails (and in turn, saving all that review time and brain cycles), I direct them to this webpage and ask them to pick a time that works for both of us. No more back and forth e-mails for either of us. This is especially helpful when working with larger groups. I prefer this method as well when trying to schedule meetings with others. I can usually set up a meeting with all the necessary confirmations in two minutes or less.

"I'm sorry, but I have to move this afternoon's meeting back to yesterday morning. Is that good for you?"

The third benefit of sharing calendars is that other people can subscribe as well. Just like I mentioned before, you can subscribe to other people's calendars and see what events are happening. So if you create a calendar for upcoming events or organizations, the only thing you have to do is have others subscribe to it. They will automatically receive updates on their own calendars. This saves everyone a tremendous amount of time. There's no need to exchange e-mails regarding upcoming events. It will automatically show on their calendars. Remember, you can show or hide these calendars as you wish.

"But everyone at work uses Exchange®. Can they still see my stuff?" Good question.

Yes! Syncing your calendar with your work calendar has never been easier. Google provides tools to sync with Outlook®, iCal®, Android®, Blackberry®, iPhone®, or your windows mobile device. Additionally, there are different Web-optimized versions you can access any type of device that can get online. For more information check:

http://www.google.com/support/calendar/bin/topic.py?topic=15305

Task Integration

I mentioned before that Google Tasks integrates nicely with Google Calendar. Any task that you add in Gmail can easily be accessed by clicking the task button on the left-hand side at the top. A new window on the right-hand side similar to listing Gmail will appear on the right.

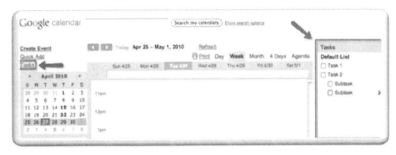

It's a great way to see what's going on today and work on your tasks at the same time. If you've assigned due dates to your items, they'll also appear at the top of your calendar as all-day events with boxes to check off the item that you should do as well. If you need to move an item to another day, you can simply click and drag it to another day, and it will move the item and assign a new due date.

Typical day workflow

Calendar doesn't play as an important role in my day as my Google Tasks does. I take a look at my calendar at the beginning of each day to see what free time I have. It gives me the ability to visualize my day so that I know what things I need to work on next and how long I have to work on them. I also make a value judgment so I can focus on getting the things done that I know I have time for.

For me, Google Calendar is really beneficial for sharing my calendar with my wife, my colleagues, and my clients. It really helps to arrange meetings quickly and keeps my life organized so I can focus on actually getting things done, rather than worrying about what needs attention and due dates. It is also fantastic for getting information out there to others who need my help.

Part III: Other *GOOGLE'LIZE* Tools

Chapter 6: Additional Google Tools

Google is constantly coming out with new tools to help manage information and get things done. (Once again, you can keep up with the latest at http://googlelize.com.) Almost all, if not all, of Google tools subscribe to the *GOOGLE'LIZE Your Life* philosophy of simplicity, ubiquity, and collaboration. In this chapter, I'd like to introduce a couple of tools briefly that may help you to be more productive.

Google Reader

If there are websites that you often need to reference or like to reference because it's important to you and your values, the best way to get that information is not through e-mail but rather to subscribe to an RSS reader. RSS stands for Really Simple Syndication and is a technology that allows you to get updates from websites whenever they add new content to the site. These updates can come in the form of e-mail or can be read in an e-mail like inbox.

Google Reader is currently considered to be the industry standard for these RSS readers. Almost all websites allow you to subscribe to them. Depending on your browser, you can
The RSS symbol Looks like this:
look up at the address bar and you may see an RSS icon, or a little orange symbol to the right of the address. If you click on that icon or just copy the link, you can go to Google Reader and click the "subscribe button." Add the URL you copied before and any time new content is published on that site, it shows up in your Google Reader inbox. It is like e-mail for the web.

You can go now and subscribe to our blog at http://googlelizing.com. Just look for the RSS symbol in the top next to the address bar, or look for the orange symbol in the column.

I have found RSS readers useful for keeping up with family and friends as they update their personal blogs and websites. This is important to me, so I make it a priority to read these things often. I also find it useful for research and keeping up with what's going on in the news. By using Google Reader, I've eliminated a lot of information that used to hit my e-mail inbox.

A word of caution about information overload: Remember, there are millions and millions of sites out there which means that you can subscribe information from just about anywhere. Rather than fill your Google Reader with information that you don't really need, be wise in your selection and only put things in your Google Reader that are important to you. Regularly review your list of subscriptions and remove subscriptions that you are not reading. Taking time to remove them rather than simply ignoring them ultimately saves you those precious brain cycles.

Google Voice

Many of us have multiple phone numbers by which we can be reached. More often than not, we're also constantly changing mobile devices and our numbers may change. This is where Google Voice comes in very handy. Google Voice is not a telephone service; rather it's a way to consolidate all of your telephone communication by providing you with a single number that everyone can call. You can then filter calls based on groups to certain numbers, filter by time and date, and even give special groups different outgoing messages. You can easily change phone numbers if you get a new device without having to notify everyone in the world that your number's changed.

Additionally, Google Voice can transcribe all phone messages and send them to your inbox.

I find Google Voice tremendously useful as a buffer between me and the outside world. Too often in our society, we drop everything we're doing for phone calls. Google Voice allows me to turn off all phone calls for a period of time or have them all sent to my inbox by default. I can then quickly glance at my inbox when processing e-mails and decide what information is important. The people who need to reach me know my direct line to bypass Google Voice. The rest the world gets my Google Voice number and are treated like any other message that I process in my inbox. If I can respond in two minutes or less, I'll call. If not, I add it to my list for later. I've often found that I can also just as easily respond via e-mail which I prefer.

Google Docs – Documents, Spreadsheets, Presentations, Forms, and Drawings

Google Docs is one of the most useful productivity tools. It not only allows you to create documents, spreadsheets, presentations, forms, and drawings, but also backs up all your data instantly so that you never lose it again – thus saving you hours and hours of painful backup and restoration time. The best part is that it is free, not $500 for a license like some other products out there.

In addition to being able to create documents, spreadsheets, presentations, forms, and drawings you can access your documents on any computer in the world and even mobile devices (ubiquity). There are also a myriad of sharing options for you to help you collaborate in business and your personal life. Let me share a few personal case studies.

I use **Google Docs** for collaboration on projects, writing, and planning. For example, this year my wife and I are putting together a small book of parenting tips for my brother and sister-in-law as they're having their first baby. We created a document in Google Docs and shared it with each other. I worked on it when I had a chance, and my wife did the same. We could leave each other comments within the document, and review each other's work.

I use **Google Spreadsheets** to keep track of finances and other business expenses. I share this document my wife so that she can also see our financial snapshot and add her own expenses. At any given time, we can both view the spreadsheets on our phones and even edit them in real time. I also use spreadsheets to keep track of consulting hours, expenses and billing that I share with my accountant.

I use **Google Presentations** whenever I give a presentation. It allows me not only to collaborate if I have a co-presenter but also to share the presentation with others during and after the presentation easily. There is also a URL to which you can direct people to make it easy for them to see what you're seeing and add questions in the comments section. You can give participants access to navigate around to other parts of the presentation while you give it as well.

Google Forms is the next component in the Google Docs suite. Forms allows people to create custom, online forms that they can share via a URL and collect responses. These forms can be used for surveys, gathering information, guest books, or a myriad of other options. It interfaces with the Google Spreadsheet which updates every time anyone submits a new form. These forms can also be embedded on Web pages and easily shared. I once used forms to gather letters to my wife for her birthday. I simply sent out a URL with a link to the form. Rather than correlate all the responses, they just went into a spreadsheet that I then merged into a document to create a book for her.

Google Docs is one of the areas in which Google has been doing a lot of innovating. They are constantly adding newer features and recently added **Google Drawings**. It is an application that lets you draw complex drawings with shapes. It's great for organizational charts or to plan the layout for events such as a wedding. In addition, when you are working on a document with someone else, you can see what they're typing as they type it. It's a good way to avoid wasting time as you brainstorm, revise, or compose documents in real time.

To find more tips for getting started with Google Docs, or ideas on how to *GOOGLE'LIZE* your documents, spreadsheets, and presentations be sure to check out http://Googlelize.com. All these tools are designed to aid the modern 'knowledge worker'. Using the Google products will save you tremendous amounts of time whether you're trying to collaborate on documents or simply trying to find them.

Google Wave is another new product. Until recently, it was an invite-only product but is now open to anyone with a Google account. Google wave is an email like program, but instead of tracking individual emails, it tracks conversations. It also has the ability to collaboratively edit waves, or these email like documents. You can see what others are typing as they edit the wave.

Google Wave certainly isn't a replacement for e-mail; I see it more as a cross between email and documents. With Google Wave you can create fantastic digital white board for collaborating online or even in person. It has the same sharing features as other Google documents. You can also go back and re-play a wave to see how people arrived at a conclusion.

I use Google Wave with groups of people. We sit around with our individual laptops, but have a common digital whiteboard where we can write all of our brainstorming ideas and have our record of our conversation for future reference. Unlike a wiki, for example, it's real-time collaboration. The ability to see what others are typing as you work on a document is a real productivity enhancer!

In the future, you'll be able to embed Google Wave on any Web page. The possibilities for collaboration are endless as there are also numerous extensions available for increasing communication. A common extension is a "what you'll bring to the party." You can embed a little poll in this collaborative email document wave that allows people to sign up for what they are bringing to a party. Once again, this eliminates dozens of e-mails from being sent back and forth as people add their own information directly to the e-mail like documents.

Chapter 7: On the Go – Mobile Devices

"E-mail, voice mail, web pages, stock quotes, news, banking...that's a lot of responsibility for such a little guy!"

Remember car phones? Maybe you're not quite old enough, but car phones were the rage "back in the day." The busiest executives all had them so that they could be reached while they were on the go. They were hard-wired and needed an antenna attached to the car. But hey, you could take or make a call from your car.

Then came cell phones. They were light years ahead of car phones – no wires and no cars needed. You could make a call from anywhere. How great was that? Need internet access? Oops...still only a phone.

Now we've got quite an assortment of "mobile devices" that let you access the Web and your entire on-line life from the palm of your hand. Wow – is that great or what? Our problems are over, right? Well, not so fast. If you're using a mobile device, you probably learned very quickly that it's critical to keep all of your devices in sync.

Meet Ted. Ted learned that lesson the hard way. He thought he was cutting edge because he could check his calendar from his mobile device; however, he didn't sync it with his desk calendar as often as he should have with disappointing results. He'd noted the meeting time change on his desktop calendar but never sync'd his mobile device. He ended up hanging out at the coffee place until 10:00 because according to his calendar, the meeting started at 10:30. Ted forgot that the time was changed to 9:30 – duly noted on his desktop calendar, but Ted wasn't at this desk. He relied on the stale information stored on his phone.

Our ultra-productive friend, Bob, understands and takes the time to keep everything in sync. Bob showed up at the meeting right on time and was awarded the project and the raise. Ted was sipping a latte. Sue? Sue's still too busy trying to find the meeting information in her e-mail to even consider using a mobile device.

Too Many Devices?

There are a lot of smart phones on the market. A browse through the aisles at an electronics big-box store validates that statement. There are features galore, so which one is best?

First things first (again): If you're ready to jump into the smart phone market or are looking to change or upgrade your device, the first thing to look for is comfort. Pick a device that you're comfortable using. Is it easy for you to carry around, use, and read? Never mind the hype and what's deemed coolest. If you're not comfortable using it, you're not going to be productive, and in my book, productivity trumps cool every time. You want a phone that lets you do all your productive work easily and efficiently. Ted likes to be cool; Bob understands the importance of "form follows function," and after all, Bob just got the raise!

Ted's problem is that while he's comfortable with his phone, it doesn't sync easily, so he doesn't take the time to keep all of his information up-to-date on all his devices. Bob has *Google'lized his life*, so syncing is a no-brainer for him.

Google syncs with every available mobile device. You can pick the phone you're comfortable using without worrying about whether it will be supported to do the things you need and want to do. If you *GOOGLE'LIZE Your Life,* you can be ahead of the curve and eliminate a lot of syncing issues. I've used the iPhone® for several years and currently use an android phone. It syncs even better with Google stuff and keeps me at the top of my productivity. (What can I say? I'm a Google fan!) I also now have a 3G iPad® for processing e-mails on the go that allows me to get online and process longer emails, edit and compose documents, and read my Google reader items easily.

Information To Go

The role of the mobile device is to keep up with your information while you're on the go. There are fewer and fewer "Knowledge Workers," who sit at their desks all day long. Having "on-the-go" access to your productivity system will become more important with every passing month and year. Besides, do you *want* to sit at your desk all day?

With the right mobile device and a good productivity system, you can work from anywhere. With that ability, comes the ability to take better control of your time, and controlling your time is really what productivity is all about – having the time to do what's important to you based on your value system.

If you can turn unproductive time into time to get things done, you'll ultimately have more time for yourself. I often put off things that I know I can easily do on my phone for what would otherwise be unproductive times like sitting on the bus or waiting in line.

Our friend, Bob used his phone to address some last minute issues during his commute home on public transportation. He got to his son's baseball game in time to see the first pitch. Ted was stuck at his desk because his phone couldn't support his productivity system. He got to the game in the fourth inning. Sue? Forget it...she never made it to the game since she wasted two hours during the day looking for e-mails.

Device Breakdown

Mobile devices are as varied as computers. Everyone has a favorite. The two most important features for most people are wireless carrier and cost. If you have a carrier that you've been with for years and your family is with them as well, chances are you aren't going to change, so look at what types of phones they offer.

Here's my (probably a bit biased) breakdown of the most popular smart phones (or phones that have the ability to add applications, access your e-mail, and access the Internet).

First Smartphone Warning

If this is your first Smartphone, there is something you need to know: Most, if not all, Smartphones require a data connection. So in addition to the $100-$500 price for the device you can expect to pay an extra $30-$50/month to your phone bill.

Also, be prepared to spend some time learning about your device. Just like it takes time to learn the shortcuts, it takes time to get to know a new device. Set aside some time to get your device set up. I usually know that when I get a new mobile device, I should plan at least a day out of my schedule to get it up and running. You'll want to get everything set up at once and get your system running like a well-oiled machine.

Most important is to make sure you can access your HUB from your device. With that said, let's talk about the options that are out there and how you might *GOOGLE'LIZE* your mobile device.

Popular Models: Nexus 1® (T-Mobile only), Verizon Motorola Droid®, Verizon Incredible®, HTC Hero® (T-Mobile), EVO (Sprint).

I sport the Droid® and love it. It has an on-screen keyboard across the whole device that allows me to trace letters instead of typing each one individually. This tracing keyboard is called a shapewriter keyboard. It's by far the easiest-to-use mobile device keyboard there is. This is important if you want to be productive and respond to e-mails while you're on the go. It also has a physical keyboard that slides out for those who like a little bit more of a physical touch.

One of the great things about the Droid® device is the built-in Gmail client, complete with all my contacts and conversation view. Set up is super fast and syncs all Google Calendars. There are also a growing number of applications including a great free one called gTasks which shows me all my tasks, and even puts a nice little short screen of my "Today" tasks right on my front screen so I can keep them in mind.

It can also sync up with Exchange® and other corporate calendar and e-mail clients.

At this time, the only carrier that supports the iPhone is AT&T® although there have long been rumors of versions for other carriers like Verizon® and Sprint®.

I have used an iPhone® for the past couple of years and love it as well. It is sleek and beautiful, but as they say, the coverage is a bit lacking.

The iPhone® has no physical keyboard, but the touch keyboard is pretty good for thumb typing in landscape mode (when you turn it on its side).

The applications you can get for the device are incredible –polished, clean, and a lot to choose from. The best one for productivity in this system is GeeTasks ($1.99 at the writing of this book). It syncs up with Google Tasks, lets you move items around and to different task lists. GeeTasks also works offline as well as online.

Syncing on the iPhone® works pretty well. You sync it up through exchange and get all of your Google Calendars very easily. It's a bit harder to set up than the Android devices, but works like a charm once you get it set up. It also syncs up well with normal exchange environments and other e-mail accounts.

The built-in mail program does not support conversation view like Gmail does, and you have to manually move your e-mails to an archive folder. You can, of course, go to an online iPhone® optimized version of Gmail through the browser, but it's slower compared to the local mail client.

The iPad® has the same functionality as the iPhone® as far as capabilities go, but it has a whole lot more screen space. That really makes a difference when you want to be productive. The more screen space you have, the easier it is to do work. You can type with two hands on the iPad®, and the online Gmail interface is surprisingly like the regular browser experience. With a 3G connection you can really get some stuff done.

Blackberry®

AT&T®, T-Mobile®, and Verizon® all have Blackberry® devices. The most popular devices are the Curve series and the Bold series.

Blackberries® are known for catering to the business crowd. Although other devices are making their way in, the business world is still dominated by Blackberry® users. They were the first real business getting email on the go and mobile productivity.

Most companies have a Blackberry® server that syncs up all their corporate mail.

Blackberry® devices are also known for their physical keyboard. Some business executives can type at lightning speed on those devices.

I had a Blackberry® for several years, and there's a great Gmail application that is fast and supports all your Gmail features like archive and threaded view. They also have a very nice Gmail calendar sync application that will sync up your calendars with your built-in Blackberry® calendar.

The big downside for this productivity system is that, as of the writing of this book, there is no way to access your Google Tasks on your Blackberry® except through a Web interface. While that works, it's not ideal if you don't have a good Internet connection. And as I have mentioned before, if it's even a little bit hard, you will give up on it.

Windows® Mobile Devices

This is where the devices really start to explode, and there are no clear leaders. All carriers also have devices that run Windows Mobile®. Some popular ones include the Samsung Omnia®, the T-Mobile HTC HD2®, the Sprint Intrepid®, the Verizon HTC Imagio®.

These devices are most similar to an Android device in that they have the shapewriter keyboard installed, and many of them also have keyboards that you can use. Recently they've come out with many iPhone'esqe touch screen devices as well with on-screen keyboards.

Because they are Windows® devices, they sync seamlessly with business exchange environments. They also sync with Gmail and Google Calendar just fine through ActiveSync. Google has created conduits for this that can be downloaded for free.

As with the Blackberry®, the only way to currently access Google Tasks is through an online Web interface.

Chapter 8: Small g - *'google'lized'* Tools

There are other tools available that fall into the simplified, collaborative, and ubiquitous access *GOOGLE'LIZE Your Life* mantra.

Flash Readers

The average adult reads around two words per second, or 120 words per minute.[3] I was really skeptical speed readers that say they can read up to 1000 words a minute. I decided that it was worth the time to explore this option to determine if it was actually true. I quickly found out that although it's possible to read faster, it takes a lot of discipline. Unless you have something to help you stay focused on what you are reading, you'll often get distracted and drop back into your regular reading habits.

The real idea behind speed-reading is that you stop vocalizing the words on the page. Most of the time, when you read you say, or vocalize, the words in your mind. But, our minds are much more capable than that and can process a lot more information than we often give it credit for. This is where flash readers come into play.

Flash readers allow you to copy text and paste it into a reader that will flash chunks of text in front of your eyes for you automatically. You can set the speed so that it goes only as fast as you want it to go, but you can easily read three or four times faster using this method. There is no need for you to learn speed reading techniques. You can paste the text in you want to read, set the speed, and read. I routinely read articles around 800 words per minute. This is really one of those technologies that need to be experienced

---

[3] "Speed Reading" - http://en.wikipedia.org/wiki/Speed_reading.

to be understood. Be sure to go to http://Googlelize.com to see an example of how this all works.

There's always the danger of losing comprehension when you read items faster. For that reason, I usually only use this technology when I'm trying to read something that I have to read but may not be that important to me. I almost never use it to read letters from friends and family, or if I do, I slow the speed way down so that my comprehension stays high. However, it is very helpful for articles, long memos, and long business e-mails that you know you need to read but don't want to.

There are several tools available to assist in flash reading. Here are a couple free ones that I like:

- Zap reader® – this is an online tool that has a neat little bookmark you can add to your browser. Then all you have to do is select the text that you want to speed-read and click the bookmark to open up a new window – http://www.zapreader.com/
- WordFlashReader® – This is a standalone PC client that allows you to read text while you're off-line as well – http://wordflashreader.sourceforge.net/
- iReadFast® – Off-line Mac/Linux client – http://gengis.110mb.com/en/index.php

Text-to-speech

Both PC and Mac operating systems have built-in text-to-speech capabilities. They basically take any text that you copy and read it to you out loud. More often than not, the voice is mechanical, but it is still quite understandable, and it can save you a tremendous amount of time if you need to multitask. I often use this function to "read" articles as I work out.

You can access the speech-to-text engine on a PC by going to "start – control panel – speech." Here's a good article for troubleshooting and getting text to speech set up on your computer as well: http://support.microsoft.com/kb/306902.

You can access the speech-to-text engine on the Mac by going to "system preferences – speech – text-to-speech."

There are also text-to-speech programs for mobile devices like the iPhone® which allow you to listen to stuff on the go.

Speech-to-text

"We need better speech-recognition software. I told my employees to celebrate their diversity. The computer thought I said 'perversity'!"

There are technologies now available that allow you to speak to a computer and have it "write down" the words that you're saying. This technology has been around for a while, but in recent years it has become more accurate and more readily available.

When you first start the program, you train it to listen to your voice. It takes about 15 minutes to set up and get started. Over time, as it gets phrases wrong, you can train it further. After a few weeks, you'll notice you have to fix fewer and fewer mistakes. The time investment in this case has paid off for me.

While it's good for long documents and longer e-mails, I've found that it's not helpful for shorter items that I can quickly type myself. Processing e-mail, for example, is much faster when I use the keyboard and keyboard shortcuts to reply to e-mails quickly.

I must say, however, that I do love sitting back, relaxing, and just talking to the computer to be more productive. Or sometimes standing up and walking around the room while I dictate get the creativity juices flowing.

On the PC, there's a program called Dragon Speak®. It's about $80. I use MacSpeech Dictate® and it costs about $150.

Evernote®

Sometimes keeping your life organized does not fit in the confines of your task list. I try to put as much in my hub as possible, but that does not  always work. Evernote (http://evernote.com) at its core is a note taking application. You can create huge documents, and add them to categories. Additionally, you can take photos and upload them as a note, record audio, even upload PDF's and other documents. It is really another hub for all your information. Some people actually use Evernote® as the hub for all info, and put their task lists inside of a note. Not a bad idea at all if it works for you.

There are a variety of ways you can access the notes. There is the online version, mobile device applications, and local Mac and PC programs. It just so happens that I'm typing this portion of the book on a plane right now, and earlier today, I jotted down some things I wanted to add to this book while I was working on my iPad®. It synced everything up and pulled a local copy onto my computer which I am able to access here. Pretty neat stuff.

Evernote® is a classic Freemium service (i.e. they offer a great service for free, and have a premium update with more features). You can upload up to 40MB of data for free each month, and upgrade and upload up to 500MB each month for $5/month. Because I primarily use text notes I have never come close to my 40MB free limit.

Doodle.com®

One of the most frustrating and complicated things to do is set up a meeting with multiple people. E-mails go back and forth and fill up your inbox quickly. I've found a fantastic alternative tool: Doodle.com®.

Doodle® allows you to set up a Web page and display possible times when you would like to meet.

You then send a link to all the people that you would like to attend the meeting, and they enter the times when they're available. Only one e-mail needs to be sent out announcing it and one declaring what time you'll meet. I use it on a regular basis to get people together. After everyone has responded (you get notified whenever anyone does add their available times, but be sure to set up a filter for this so you can just look when it is done), you can go in and easily see when the best time to meet is. It saves you tons of e-mails!

Other tools

Any tool that allows you to simplify your life, collaborate online, and is accessible in many different ways can help you *GOOGLE'LIZE Your Life*. I'm only scratching the surface as far as other available productivity tools go, and more and more people are getting the idea now. It seems that every week someone invents another great product that really can save some time.

To share your ideas, or to find the latest time saving tools, be sure to go to the *GOOGLE'LIZE your Life* website at http://Googlelize.com.

Part 4: Practice

Chapter 9: A Day in my Life

I've given you a lot of information about how you can improve your productivity by *GOOGLE'LIZING Your Life,* and I'd like to share how I put all of this into play. I've been telling you throughout the book about how much time I save, so now I'll show you specifically.

Again, you will need to take some time to get things set up and transition to a new style of working (more on that in the next chapter), but I guarantee that once you make the conversion, the initial investment of your time will pay off handsomely.

Daily

Before work/on the way to work:

After I wake up I check e-mail while I'm getting ready for the day. However, I don't check email on my computer – only on my mobile device so I won't be tempted to get distracted. This is when I read the news and Facebook® items. This is also when I pull items from my "This Week" task list onto "Today" list for the most important items of the day if I didn't do so the day before.

Morning:

The first thing I do in the morning when I start work is to look at my today task list inside my hub. I have a good idea of what I'm going to work on before I get to work because I've reviewed it and prioritized the top things on my list the day before. DO NOT open e-mail!

12:00:

I process e-mail at noon by responding to e-mails that I can do in two minutes or less; putting calendar items on my calendar with detailed information in the description so I don't have to look for it later (no wasted brain cycles);

and adding the rest of the emails as tasks on in my hub. Remember your values in this section. Think about what is most important to you as you process these emails. Don't put things on your calendar or in your hub that you will not do. Focus, focus, focus on the most important things to *you*.

Before lunch, I make decisions about time frames for the items I've just added to my task list and put them into "Today" (now meaning this afternoon), "This week," "Next week," or one of my context lists.

12:30 Lunch:

During lunch I usually read some Facebook® updates; watch a video or two on my phone; socialize with real human beings for once! Remember that you need to unstring the bow every once in a while so it doesn't lose its spring. The same is true for each of us. We need that down time, and if we don't take it when it comes, we'll take it when we could otherwise be productive.

1:00:

After lunch I head back to my hub and continue work on the tasks for the day. If I run out of tasks I will pull tasks from "This Week" list.

4:00 Process E-mail:

Just before the end of the day I will process e-mail one more time. Additionally, I take this time to organize my hub by prioritizing my task list for the next day by moving items to different lists as needed.

Night:

During the night I try not to check e-mail at all, or check infrequently on my mobile device so I can focus on the most important things at home.

(If you have a job that requires you to work at night, I recommend that you take a 5:00-6:00 break and then be productive from 6:00-9:00 before checking e-mail again.)

Weekly and Long Term

On Monday mornings, I like to take 30 minutes at the beginning of my day to just go through my hub and pull items from my "Long Term" context lists and put them on my "This Week" list. I also put tasks on my "Long Term" context list that I can't work on now.

I also review my long-term goals once a month on the first Monday of the month. I take this time to really take a step back for a few minutes to take a look at how life is going, the tasks I am doing, and how those fit in with what is important to me and my long term personal and professional goals.

Chapter 10: Getting Started!

Okay, so now you understand the importance of *GOOGLE'LIZING Your Life*, and you understand the theories and the tools. I certainly hope you agree with the importance of controlling your technology in order to be productive rather than letting it control you. You know how ridiculous it is to let the tail wag the dog!

You're ready to go but worried about making the change. In this chapter, I'll provide a step-by-step guide to facilitate your conversion. I can't do it for you – in fact, no one can, but I'll try to make this the next-best thing.

You can apply any one part of the system at a time. Don't put off applying the most important things you have learned so far waiting until you have everything. Small and simple changes make all the difference.

Choosing Your Tools

First, you've got to decide: paper or digital? If you need a review of the pros and cons of each option, head on back to Chapter 1.

Next, decide if you can use Google or an outside resource. Depending on the culture of your company, this decision may already be made for you. For many, Outlook/Exchange® is the default system. The most important thing is to be unified with your productivity system. You must be able to access it from anywhere. And it should certainly follow the three tenets I preached about in the beginning: Easy, ubiquitous, flexible.

Hub:

Pick your hub. Remember, this is your central gear, and everything else will move based on this one thing. Give some thought to your hub choice. (Review Chapter 4 again, if needed, before you make your selection.) Rushing through choosing and setting up your hub can lead to disappointment with your productivity system. It needs to be simple and flexible so that you won't give up on it in a few weeks after the novelty of your new system has worn off.

Next, set up the categories in your hub:

- Set up time-frame categories
- Set up context categories
- Start putting some things in there. Remember to make a values judgment before it goes into your hub. Is this really important enough to go in here, or is it just wishful thinking?
- Print out shortcuts, and place them next to your screen

E-mail:

Take a deep breath. Now's the time to decide if you really want to declare e-mail bankruptcy. (Give Chapter 5 another look if you're not sure.) At the very least, pick a date (not longer than one month prior) and process only those e-mails into your hub or on to your calendar. Remember: The goal is "Inbox Zero."

- Look for rules to apply to clean up your inbox
- Set up e-mail policy; notify those that need to know.
- Set up signature or auto -response

Once you have set up your e-mail and your tasks, try it out for a day or even half a day. Remember when I said that e-mail was an addiction? That makes it especially hard to stop checking e-mails every time a task gets hard or you have a spare minute. Try to close out your e-mail completely for a while and work on your tasks.

When you re-open your e-mail, try to process your e-mail, and resist the urge to start building up your task list in your inbox again. Try to process your e-mail as quickly as possible and get it closed again so you can focus on tasks.

112

Calendar:

Export the critical information from your current calendar, and get everything into a single, unified calendar. Again, this isn't going to happen overnight, and you will probably spend a few days or a couple weeks working back and forth between systems.

- Set up repeating events
- Set up sharing, and subscribe to most common calendars.

Mobile Device:

I would recommend you find someone with a device like the one you are thinking of getting and play with it for a while (as long as they will let you). When it comes to mobile devices, you really have to feel comfortable with the input methods. One of the nice things about Google is that it will sync up with just about anything.

Once you decide on your phone and make the purchase, you will initially need to do the following:

- Set up Gmail (or E-mail account)
- Set up Syncing (Over the air sync is best)
- Find a way to access your tasks (download program, or bookmark tasks on your front screen)

Other Google Services:

Take a look at the other *GOOGLE'LIZE Your Life* tools:

- Download a local flash reader program, or put the ZapReader bookmarklet in your toolbar. Test read a longer article to see how you like it.

- Subscribe to the websites that you visit most often in your Google Reader
- Test the text-to-speech capability on your computer to see how you like it.

Test it all out!

Now is the time when it all comes together. Give it a try. Test it out. Again, start by implementing one idea, and get really comfortable with that. Don't know which one to start with? Think about the low-hanging fruit: Where you do feel you waste the most time in your day with technology? Apply that first. I highly recommend getting your inbox clean and implementing the two-minute rule.

Once you've got that under your belt, try applying more and more as you go along. Hone and configure your system over time. Try things out and find out what works best for you.

Let me reiterate the importance of putting this into place piece by piece. If you make it too overwhelming, you set yourself up for failure. Yes, it's going to take an investment of time on your part to initially get underway when you *GOOGLE'LIZE Your Life*. Keep in mind that time spent initially is an investment, and it will pay off in the long run.

Let's look at the people we've met throughout the book and see how they've fared:

First, there's Sue. Good ol' Sue. She's not a bad person or a bad worker. She means well and is loyal to her company. Sue's real problem is that she is afraid of change, change of any type, large or small, and it's fear that makes her unproductive. It was a quantum leap for Sue to begin using e-mail, and she probably wouldn't have if she had not been forced to do so. Sue's also afraid of losing what she thinks is valuable information and data, so she never deletes anything. The problem is that more information constantly streams into her inbox. She can't stop it, and she's completely lost control.

My first suggestion for Sue would be to move every e-mail that's older than a month or two into her archive, or all-mail folder. She should then begin learning to use the search tool in her e-mail client to get to old messages, if she needs them at all. She can sleep better at night knowing the information is still there *if* she needs it. She can then begin to use a task hub she's created to keep track of her work and create a new habit.

After all, we're all creatures of habit.

What unproductive habits have you formed over the years working with technology? Like Sue, I encourage you to change those habits today and establish a better, more efficient, more productive working style!

Next there's Ted. Unlike Sue, Ted loves technology. However, Ted's been too quick to grab and try every new thing that's come along. He's got a little of everything on several different platforms. Ted's biggest problem is that he *thinks* he's productive because he's using all this technology. In reality, Ted wastes a lot of time manually moving things from his e-mail to his calendar to his task list. Besides wasting time, Ted also opens the door for human error with this approach. Remember Ted sipping the latte and missing the meeting? That was just the tip of his proverbial iceberg. Ted's always dropping the ball – making errors by manually coordinating all his incoming information. Of course, Ted blames technology, but his colleagues understand that technology only does what we tell it to do.

You may be a bit like Ted. After all, every day "there's a new app for that", and we're all encouraged by friends, colleagues and sharp advertising executives to jump on board. If you fail to make your various technologies work together, you remain a slave to machines rather than the other way around. Ask yourself: How many times is the tail wagging your dog?

Finally, there's Bob. While Bob may have inherited the "productivity" gene from his great-grandfather, he also knows that everyone can *learn* to be more productive. He isn't afraid to ask for help when it comes to understanding and learning new technology. He knows that there are a lot of people just like him who need help but who muddle through on their own instead or pretend that they know how to use technology best. Bob knows Ted very well.

Bob's also taken the time to make certain that his technologies are working well together and interacting with each other with a click or a drag-and-drop. Bob's great-grandfather taught him that machines are meant to make life easier. The cars that Robert helped assemble allowed folks to get from one place to another faster and easier. How much benefit would those cars have been if owners spent ten minutes fixing them for every minute they actually drove from point A to point B? None at all.

Today's technology is no different. Do you spend ten minutes tinkering for every minute that you use your computer to do actual work? I encourage you to be like Bob and make certain that the technology you're using is, in fact, making your life easier by making you more productive.

I want you to *GOOGLE'LIZE Your Life* starting now so that you can reach the meaningful goals you set for yourself and do what is most important to you.

Made in the USA
Lexington, KY
03 July 2012